Horses That Buck

Horses That Buck

The Story of Champion Bronc Rider Bill Smith

Margot Kahn

UNIVERSITY OF OKLAHOMA PRESS : NORMAN

For Bill and Carole,
for Scott,
and for all my family

Library of Congress Cataloging-in-Publication Data

Kahn, Margot, 1978–
    Horses that buck : the story of champion bronc rider Bill Smith /
Margot Kahn.
        p. cm. — (Western legacies series ; v. 5)
    Includes bibliographical references and index.
    ISBN 978-0-8061-3912-8 (hardcover : alk. paper)   1. Smith, Bill,
1941 June 28–   2. Bronc riding.   3. Rodeos.   I. Title.
    GV1834.45.B75C38 2008
    791.8'4092—dc22
    [B]
                                                    2007032399

Horses That Buck: The Story of Champion Bronc Rider Bill Smith
is Volume 5 in The Western Legacies Series.

The paper in this book meets the guidelines for permanence and
durability of the Committee on Production Guidelines for Book
Longevity of the Council on Library Resources, Inc. ∞

2 3 4 5 6 7 8 9 10

Contents

Illustrations

Preface

Even the skinniest man is handsome on horseback. He is handsomer still when he wears his hat down low, when his eyes—especially if they are steel blue—are set deep, and when the skin of his face is carved in sharp crow's feet and in soft curves around the mouth. A thin man often has beautiful hands, if they are working hands, or so I have found, but if he is working, his hands may be gloved and so they will be mysterious. His legs, which may be storklike, are purposeful when mounted, wrapped with strength around the belly of a horse, and his nonexistent rear is obscured in the seat of his saddle.

This was how I first saw Bill Smith, on a little gray, a flag in his hand. The first thing I heard him say was, "There are two things in this world I would fight to the death for," and I noticed how easy he was sitting in his saddle, how his eyes shone under the shadow of his hat, how the heels of his hands rested on his saddle horn. The gathered crowd leaned or sat on the rails of the round pen and shifted in the heat. When the gray shifted, the saddle creaked. He said the two things he would fight for were his wife and his freedom, in that order. I looked around for his wife, but none of those assembled looked the least bit likely. I turned back to my horse and tightened the cinch, exchanged the halter for a bridle, and listened as my horse did, with one ear, to this man. He spoke of freedom and of companionship, of animal instinct, of will and determination, of strength and loyalty, of generosity, gratitude, and reverence. The words he used were plain. He said that if, one day, all the horses had to leave this world, he would go with them. I swung myself into the saddle and turned up the road.

That afternoon, my mother sat in the sun behind the lodge and painted the surrounding mountain vistas, while my father and brother angled for rainbow trout. We had converged at the Home Ranch in Clark, Colorado, for our annual family vacation. The same week, the ranch had hired Bill Smith to train green colts in the mornings and to ride with the wranglers and guests in the afternoons. It was said he was a master horseman and had a gentle approach toward training, riding, and dealing with horses. I had never heard of him or his method before. But the day after I overheard his speech in the round pen, he brought his coffee and sat down next to me at lunch. He didn't say much, just "I think I'll come and set here with you." His body almost curled into the low chair as he settled into it, completely relaxed, as if to show that the chair demanded nothing of him physically, and he cradled his coffee as if there wasn't enough of it. I rode with him that afternoon and the next, and the day after that.

On Friday night we ate an early dinner and went into town for the rodeo. The Steamboat Springs Night Rodeo is small potatoes as far as rodeos go, but I had nothing to compare it with; it was the first rodeo I had ever seen. We climbed high into the bleachers and found spots in the sun, but Bill and his wife, Carole, kept moving. They got up and hovered over the chutes to watch the inside action, stood down near the fences by the judges. Carole wore a red jacket that said "Bill Smith" in cursive across the back; she was almost as tall as he, and slim. They kept close to each other, holding hands carefully, like they were on a date. Girls on fast horses made laps of the arena carrying flapping flags, clowns kicked their boots in the arena dust, and as the evening grew bitingly cold, the lights came up.

When Bill finally returned to the stands, he couldn't sit still. He said it wasn't a very good rodeo, that the judges were inflating the markings; he said that he wasn't much of a rodeo fan anyway, never could get used to watching it from the stands. But there was something about the way he watched the proceedings, especially the men who rode the bucking broncs, and there was a distant but competitive edge in his voice. I did not know then that he had spent twenty years on the road, riding under the lights of arenas full of cheering fans. I did not know how much work it took him to get there, or how many sleepless nights, flat tires, and broken bones. I did not know how many miles he traveled for the chance to ride a horse that bucked, or what it felt like, or how the road could make you feel free. Later someone said to me, "You know, Bill's a three-time world champion bronc rider." Someone else said, "Bill, he's lived a life most people only dream about—and some people wouldn't dream of."

The next morning I had to leave. I said goodbye to my family, and then I found Bill walking with his horse toward the round pen. I said, "I've come to say goodbye."

"Well, hold on," he said, stopping his horse and stepping off, draping the reins loosely over his forearm. He said, "Let me shake your hand." The little horse stood patiently while we exchanged a few words. He said I should come and visit his ranch whenever I was in Thermopolis, the chances of which I thought were highly unlikely. Not wanting to let go of the opportunity, I said, "I'd like to write a book about you."

Bill said, "Well, I'd like to help you in any way that I can. But I don't know what you're going to write about."

U

Three months later, I flew into Cody. There was snow in the mountains, and the sky was streaked with mare's tails. Carole met me at the airport, and we ate lunch at the airport café. Eyeing my grilled ham and cheese, Carole said, "Bill was worried you might be one of those vegetarians." She then took me to meet Bill's mother, his sister Barbara Reid, his niece Lori Coy, and a family friend. Over several pots of coffee in Bill's mother's living room, the women told stories about their Bill Smith. Ignorant of how it might make them nervous, I ran my tape recorder and scribbled notes in my notebook, and in the end the tape was blank because I did not know how to work my first tape recorder. At dusk, Carole and I drove eighty miles to Thermopolis in her white Ford F-250. We had the road to ourselves and did not see much of anything except for one quiet, small town.

The Smith ranch sits on two hundred acres in a bend of the Bighorn River. Alfalfa is harvested in the spring and summer while the horses pasture close to the water; in winter the horses run everywhere. The main house is a double-wide trailer at the end of a long, rutted road, only sometimes accessible without four-wheel drive. The house is surrounded by outbuildings, a barn with stalls for six horses, a hay shed, an indoor arena, and several pastures. Inside, a master bedroom, a guest bedroom, and an office branch off the main living room and kitchen. The guest room looks out onto the satellite dish, the pastures, the long drive that runs along the train tracks, and the neon light of the Super 8 Motel over the hill on the main road through town. In the alcove between the guest room and the office, the walls are covered with old black-and-white 8x10 photographs. Many are of Bill making picture rides on broncs like Sage Hen, Wall Street, and Descent. In each, the horse is caught balancing on its front hooves, its hind legs high in the air behind, suspended in motion, as if it were diving into the ground, and Bill purses his lips together, his jaw tight, his eyes focused somewhere in front of him. He sits straight up, like the pivot in the center of a seesaw, one hand on a rope rein and one hand high in the air. A few photos are of Carole and her horse, Printer, racing around a turn, dirt flying from the horse's hooves like water. And others are of their friends—Jim Houston, Joe Alexander, Mel Hyland— who have signed the photographs with thanks, best wishes, and love.

In the spare bedroom, Carole had cleared the desk and made space in the closet for me. Too tired to organize, I set my bag next to the glass gun case with its resting rifles and went to sleep. When I woke, land and sky were a blank canvas. A four-point buck left quiet cloven prints past the satellite dish outside. I watched him as I pulled on several layers of clothes. In the living room, Bill sat in his La-Z-Boy watching the news on CNN. When I emerged, he came and joined me at the kitchen table for breakfast. He sat in the chair beneath the phone, though he hates to answer it, closest to the TV, in case anything exciting should happen, with his back to the wall and with a view of the door like the Sundance Kid. It would be in that spot, over the next several years, that we would sit with notebooks and my tape recorder between us. Often the dishwasher would be humming, or the washer and dryer thumping out a rhythmic beat, sometimes both at once, almost drowning out our voices on tape. We would talk for a few hours, break for lunch, watch football, do chores, tend horses, move cattle, ride.

U

This book is not intended to be a full history of rodeo or western life; there are numerous books on these subjects, and the bibliography lists several. This is the story of a man, a life, and a period of time in the American West.

In gathering my information, I read books and watched movies; I went to rodeos in more than a few states; I traveled back and forth to Bill and Carole's ranch and to their friends' ranches and to their horse sales and clinics. I sat on a fence rail with Chuck Swanson and watched younger cowboys train two-year-old colts; I visited with Bill's nephew Jack Wipplinger and his sons, Sky and Lat, who filled me in on the annual Smith family fishing trips. I met Bill at the National Finals Rodeo in Las Vegas and followed him to the Gold Buckle Club, where the world champion cowboys gather to visit and reminisce before the nightly competitions. I talked to Clyde Frost about his son's career and his own; Jim Wise invited me to visit his saddle workshop in Loveland, Colorado, and I later did, watching for a day as he stamped leather and told me stories about traveling with Casey Tibbs. Woody Bartlett let me hang around on his Chugwater, Wyoming, ranch for a week, and Jimmy Muse let me ride his favorite horse for a few minutes. One weekend in Oklahoma City I met Larry Mahan, Clem McSpadden, Alvin Nelson, Don Harrington, Gene Peacock, and others at the National Cowboy and Western Heritage Museum. I listened to anyone who would tell me a story. I listened while stories flew around at a gathering of old friends, between riders on horseback, or across the kitchen table.

If I may make one generalization, it is that cowboys love to call one another liars. As stories are told over the years, details are embellished (the horses get wilder, the snow gets higher) and details are accumulated (someone falling off their chair upon hearing a story suddenly becomes a part of it). In fact, the more a friend is loved, the bigger liar he becomes; his sincerest compliments are in this way brushed off the humblest shoulders, and his memory is kindly called into question. In gathering stories for this book, I listened to everything and I listened to it equally, because a great story is gold, and sometimes even the most unbelievable stories are true.

In these pages, I took the threads of story I heard and the bits of history I read and turned them into narrative. I often asked several people involved in a story to tell me their version, and then I wove the versions together. In some places, I used a combination of direct quotes and imagined phrases to create dialogue in or around a scene. I felt this approach would give the reader a better sense of the action, and this style held more true to this subject than anything purely factual or more academic. In short, I took everything I heard and tried to tell a story that would give a taste of one man's life in a moment in time. I did this as accurately as I knew how, given the general fallibilities of distance and memory and the specific difficulty of interviewing subjects who, upon being asked for clarification of a point, eagerly and fondly asked me to make it up. In the end, I asked some of the subjects of this book to read it for accuracy, and they assured me that I got it just about right.

Horses That Buck

Chapter 1

All That Ever Mattered

On a hot, dry day in June 2002, at the age of sixty-one, Bill Smith rode across a high pasture in southeastern Wyoming with a string of young cowboys and me behind him. The cowboys sang songs and told jokes, gesturing gently with their hands, holding their reins loosely so they draped in soft arcs to the horses' mouths. Seventy thousand acres surrounded us in patches of dusty gold and sage. In the distance, a hundred head of Angus and Charolais speckled the plain. The cowboys had been riding all day, running for miles at a stretch, racing and playing grab-ass, trying to get one another bucked off. The horses were green, two-year-olds being ridden for the first time. At week's end, the horses would be returned to pasture until the fall, when they would be sold. Having been ridden and trained to accept a halter, bridle, saddle, and rider, they would command a premium at auction. The buyers would be horsemen, dude ranch owners, gentlemen farmers, and East Coast bankers who fancied a ride in the woods on Sunday.

We crossed the plain like a band of disorderly cavalry, and above us the clouds scattered across the sky as if they were blown out along a sheet of glass, all hovering, flat-bottomed, at the same altitude. It was Tuesday, or perhaps Wednesday; no one was keeping track. The cattle that dotted the dry pasture brought no real money; they barely paid for their own feed in a good hay year, and cost money in a bad one. The colts would bring around $1,500 each, just slightly more than the cost of raising them. The boys were working for free for the privilege of riding with Bill Smith. They considered it their summer vacation—room and board in exchange for eight hours of work a day. When the week was up, they would go back to shoeing horses, riding the rodeo circuit, or studying agriculture at one of Wyoming's community colleges. Bill would go back to his ranch, where he would focus on his own herd of horses.

As we rode, Bill looked around. He stacked his hands one on top of the other on the saddle horn. "I wonder what the poor people are doing today," he said to the horses, to the sky, to his brother, and to the young boys who were following reverently in their footsteps. The boys shrugged and snickered and rode on. The only one among them who wasn't poor was the man who owned the land, and he had made his millions investing family money in the stock market. But riding across this pasture on a weekday, they all considered themselves rich. They—the men and boys who live in double-wide trailers or out of their pickup trucks or in employers' bunkhouses—think anyone with an office job, a shift boss, or a time sheet is poor. It's the worst kind of life they can imagine.

Bill Smith is the first to admit that a man can't make a living as a cowboy anymore. But in the same breath he will declare that people will always want horses, that there will always be a market for horses no matter how industrialized our culture gets. People need animals, he thinks, to keep them human. And since he was a kid, this is what Bill Smith dreamed his life would be. "When I was a boy," he said, "I thought if you weren't a cowboy you were just underprivileged. I couldn't understand why anyone would want to be anything else."

U

When he was a boy, Bill would ride with his friend Chuck Swanson out of the valley and the town of Bearcreek, Montana, into the mountains and over the pass to Red Lodge. They would ride horses that belonged to Bill's father, Glenn, or they would ride horses they caught, horses that belonged to neighbors or friends. The town of Bearcreek had no fences, and a boy could ride any horse he could catch. Bill rarely waited for permission from anyone.

Bill Smith on his father's packhorse, ca. 1945. Collection of Bill Smith.

Bill perfected his horse-catching skills in grade school. It was a mile and a half from home to school, and in the winter, especially through deep snow, the journey was better on horseback. But most of the time Bill caught a horse to get away from school, not as a vehicle to get there. He skipped school as much as he could, riding into the mountains for the day, often with Chuck. On the many days that Bill and Chuck were caught playing hooky, the principal scolded them, saying that they would never make a living riding horses. But, Bill said, "horses was all that ever mattered to me." When it was too cold to ride, his mother, Edna, would watch him play for hours with empty glass bottles, fashioning bridles and saddles out of string and herding the bottles into corrals made of sticks.

When Bill turned nine, his father gave him a horse of his own. Glenn Smith usually bought mean horses, horses that no one else wanted, since they were the only ones he could afford. With this one relatively gentle gelding, Glenn showed Bill how a horse was broken—tied to a post, legs hobbled, exhausted until it quit fighting—a process that took hours or days, depending on the person's skill and the horse's temperament. A photograph taken a couple of years later shows the pair: an expressionless, towheaded boy seated astride a black horse with a stripe down its face.

Besides his horse, his siblings, and Chuck Swanson, Bill had few friends. He was shy and small for his age, which made him an ideal target for the bullies at school. Most days he took a beating, returning home with a bloody nose or black eye. If he was lucky he would hide in a shed or barn until after dark. On those days his mother would have to go and look for him, rescue him from his hiding place, and bring him home. The beatings, coupled with the fact that Bill had no interest in lessons and never wanted to be indoors, made his school years miserable.

In the evenings, home life was little better than the schoolyard. When Glenn came home from the bar, he had his boys practice boxing. Bill faced off against his brother Chuck, a fight he was never allowed to win. "Chuck was two years younger than me, and they would never let me hit him," Bill remembered. "They'd just let me box, and I hated that. We'd box around there, and he'd swing at me, and I'd just have to defend myself, and I'd do that for as long as I could stand it, and then I'd just hit him. Well, as soon as I did that, my dad would take the boxing gloves and he'd box me, so I wasn't going to win." For Glenn, fighting was a way of life. He and his father both were famous for bar brawls, which they often instigated and usually won. "My family, especially on my dad's side, they were all fighters," Bill said, "for as long as I can remember."

"Looking back," Bill said, "I don't know how my mother stood it." Edna cleaned the house top to bottom every day, made and mended all their clothes, and equaled or surpassed her sewing talents in the kitchen. When the chickens laid eggs, they ate eggs; when the cows gave milk, they drank milk; and when there was nothing, they ate the potatoes that the kids complained about harvesting, always trying to run off before they were made to "pick stones." If they had chickens, Edna would make fried chicken on Sundays. On Christmas they had turkey and all the trimmings; they didn't always have presents. The luxury of the Bearcreek house, while it had no bathroom, was its running water. When the children came home, filthy and exhausted, it was to a galvanized washtub and Eileen, the eldest sibling, with a scrub brush. "We might be poor," Eileen would say, "but we're gonna be clean!" Bill remembers her commanding them like a sergeant. "That was her battle cry," he said.

U

Bill celebrated his tenth birthday on June 28, 1951. That summer, like most summers in Bearcreek, meant at least one trip to the rodeo in Red Lodge, five miles over the mountains to the west. He would ride with Chuck Swanson, perhaps with his sister Barbara in hot pursuit, and they would sneak in without tickets and hide underneath the bleachers. The way Bill tells it, they would sneak under the bleachers and peer out from between the boards. From their vantage point, they could see the bucking chutes on the far side of the oval arena painted 1, 2, 3, 4, 5, 6. Behind the numbered gates, a system of fenced pens and alleys organized the horses. Above the chutes cowboys sat ready on the fence rails like birds on a wire, and above the rails the bleachers rose up to the crow's nest, where the announcer sat with a microphone and a list of contestants. But everything above and behind the chutes, everything except the numbered fences and the stretch of dirt before them, was blocked from view.

There is no way to describe exactly what happened at that rodeo in 1951, but this is how I imagine it. Boots shuffled back and forth above the boys. Peanut shells fell gently on their heads. Girls galloped around the arena to the sound of a bugle with the flags of America and Montana. The announcer welcomed the crowd, casting his voice out like a fishing line, a slow drawl quickened with excitement, landing lightly and drawing everyone's attention to the arena. And then a beautiful horse—strong-built, heavy in the hindquarters, and broad in the chest—lay himself out in long, fast strides, hugging the edge of the arena fence. A cowboy sat back in the saddle, confident and relaxed.

"Ladies and gentlemen," the announcer said, "the current world champion saddle bronc rider, steer wrestler, and all-around cowboy— born and raised right here in Red Lodge, Montana—Bill Linderman!"

The crowd jumped to its feet and cheered. Beneath the bleachers, Bill Smith yelped and punched his fist in the air.

"Watch you don't get us thrown out again," Chuck said.

"Nobody's payin' attention to us now," Bill replied, his eyes trained on Linderman.

Bill Linderman and his brother, Bud, were hometown boys who had made it big. They had left Red Lodge and its one place of employment, the coal mines, to try their luck on the road. The only thing they knew how to do was ride, so they took their saddles and drove from town to town entering every rodeo they could find. If they were lucky, which they frequently were, they would win some prize money—usually enough to buy a steak dinner, a few rounds of drinks, and enough gasoline to get to the next town. Even when they won they were as good as broke, but all they needed was to keep driving, and eventually they'd win again.

When the champion cowboys had taken their introductions and the people had taken off their hats for the national anthem, cowboys scrambled over the numbered chute gates where the horses were being loaded. "The first event of the afternoon will be the bareback bronc riding," the announcer explained. He had the smooth voice of a radio man. "Each cowboy draws a horse from the lottery before the rodeo begins, and his job this afternoon is to ride that bronc for eight seconds. If the cowboy makes it, the judges will give him a score for how well he rides. The judges will also give a score to the horse for how hard he bucks. The combined score will determine the winner." Bill and Chuck watched the chutes. In chute 2 a horse reared and pawed at the gate, his head and forefeet coming over the top rails. The cowboys clinging to the top rails skittered away and then quickly resumed their places like shooed flies. In chute 3, a cowboy was looking steady, one hand on the top rail, hat and shoulders above the fence.

"Each one of these broncs is here today because he is a wild, ornery son of a buck that just does not like to be messed with," the announcer said. "So you see, ladies and gentlemen, the predicament we have here."

Each horse in the chutes was outfitted with rigging, which amounted to a strap around the chest with a handle for the cowboy to hold. Around the horse's flanks, they strapped a sheepskin belt. Most broncs stood quiet for all this, up until a cowboy climbed over the chute and settled onto its back.

The cowboy in chute 3 had gotten this far. He nodded his head. Two men on the ground pulled the gate open and the announcer called, ". . . and out of chute three!"

A stout bay horse lunged from the gate, and the cowboy, holding the grip with one hand, set his spurs in the horse's shoulders. The horse jumped and kicked and jumped again, sinking its front feet into the sand and lifting its hindquarters high in the air. With each jump and kick he tried to dislodge the cowboy from his back, and with each jump and kick, the cowboy whipped forward and back like a switch. The cowboy held his free hand high in the air so that he would not be disqualified for touching the horse, and he waved it back and forth as if he were waving a white flag. His hat flew off on the second jump and landed in the dirt. On the fourth jump, he slipped to the left. On the fifth, he regained his balance. And on the sixth jump, he lost it completely and went flying over the horse's head. He landed solidly on his shoulder, some twenty paces from his hat. As he got up and brushed himself off, the horse bucked toward the end of the arena. Two seconds later the whistle sounded.

"Ladies and gentlemen," the announcer said, "this cowboy's only pay this afternoon is your applause." The crowd compensated him kindly, and the cowboy waved his thanks before disappearing back behind the fence.

Chute 6 was ready to go.

"Now," the announcer continued, "this next waddie broke his wrist and three ribs down in Abilene a few weeks ago, and now he's back in competition. That's called courage in my book. Let's give him a little encouragement." The announcer had gone to law school and had a handle on the language. The crowd responded to his request with applause and cheers, just as they had been asked. The kid nodded his head, the chute flew open, the horse lunged out, and the kid went flying—his hat in one direction and his body in another—to land in the dirt.

After the bareback riding, the six chute gates were closed, and the announcer directed the crowd's attention to the far end of the arena for the calf-roping event. Wrangling a calf was an impressive feat, certainly nothing Bill and Chuck could do themselves, but nothing the rodeo had to offer would hold the boys' attention as much as the saddle bronc riding, which came near the end of the program. Since they had snuck in and held no tickets, they had to stay put and hope they weren't noticed until then.

Bill was nearly champing at the bit by the time the team ropers were clearing out of the arena and the chutes were once again bustling with cowboys and horses. Each of the six chutes had two or three cowboys at the ready. One set the saddle while another fastened the flank strap. The one who was riding measured his rein, wiped his hands on his thighs, pressed his hat down low on his head, and would eventually climb over the chute rails to mount his draw. The horses that were particularly wild or those unfamiliar with the rodeo's events snorted and kicked at the chute gates. Others stood steady until they felt a cowboy hovering above them or the weight of a man on their back. The announcer watched the chutes and tried to time his banter to the activity.

"And now, ladies and gentlemen, we're moving on to the oldest event in rodeo," the announcer said. "Before a cowboy could rope a steer or catch a calf, before he could ride out a storm, before a cowboy could be a cowboy, he had to find himself a horse, and then he had to get on that horse somehow, someway. Now, in case we have any tenderfeet in the audience, allow me to remind you that horses don't come off the range ready to ride. They need to be taught that. In every batch of cowboys, there are always a few who are better at this than others, and they are called bronc busters." Bill knew this story well. He had heard it at the rodeo, and he had seen it at home. His father and his grandfather were both horsemen first, miners second, and miners only because there was no money to be made with horses anymore, unless you were a successful rodeo cowboy, and barely even then. Several cowboys flocked, ducked, and scattered from the chute on the far left. A hand rose above the fence rail to signal the gate. The cuff and sleeve were lavender.

"Out of chute number one," the announcer called, "a kid who wanted to rodeo so bad he used to lie down in the highway just to hitch a ride to the next town over. So far this year, he's the best bronc rider in the world—Casey Tibbs—out of Fort Pierre, South Dakota!" The gate swung open and a dull dun-colored horse charged out, threw his head to the right and his heels high to the left. From a distance it looked like Casey was smiling. Sitting straight up in his saddle, he held the rope rein with his right hand and waved his left hand above his head. He wore chocolate-colored chaps with his initials scripted in silver at each ankle, and he worked them up and back with the horse's movements. His timing was perfect. His balance was enviable. He made it look so easy. "You fall into a rhythm, and it's like dancing with a girl," he later explained.

It was commonly thought that Casey Tibbs had no equal in the bronc riding world, that there had never been a cowboy with such grace and charisma, with such style and charm. He was relaxed and confident and always appeared to be having fun, and he seemed to inspire the same confidence and playfulness in the horses he rode. He let every horse think that it could buck him off, so they tried harder. This was exactly what Casey wanted—a great ride, a good time, a show. When the eight-second buzzer sounded, Casey released his feet from the stirrups and ejected himself out of the saddle, over the horse's head and onto the ground in a dare-devilish leap. The crowd went wild. By 1955 he would win six world championship saddle bronc titles, a record that would not be broken in the same century.

Bill was aching with excitement. Casey had ridden well and set the bar high. A cowboy from Idaho in a plain blue shirt was up next on a notoriously difficult horse. The horse took three long leaps into the arena, each of which dislodged the kid right, left, back. On the fourth jump, the kid went over the horse's right shoulder, flailed for a moment, and landed in a heap. Although most of the audience knew the difference between a good ride and a bad one, it was exciting to see the stark contrast between a world champion and a regular professional.

Bill Linderman (*center*) and Casey Tibbs (*right*) with Deb Copenhaver, Phoenix, Arizona, 1954. Photo by DeVere Helfrich. Courtesy of the National Cowboy and Western Heritage Museum, Oklahoma City.

The poor kid from Idaho, who had been having tough luck all season, was an unfortunate but perfect example. He was strong and good-natured, but he had no natural talent. He might be a bronc rider yet, but nobody was placing bets on him.

Three more mediocre boys from Texas, Arizona, and Utah followed before an enormous figure behind gate 5 yelled, "Out!" For those who knew him, there was no mistaking Bill Linderman's frame. Six feet, two inches tall and 175 pounds, he was almost too large to ride saddle broncs. Of the Linderman boys, Bill's brother, Bud, had the natural talent. Bud was making rides on horses that nobody else could ride, and some said he was simply an artist, but people were also a bit afraid of him because he drank and fought with the same intensity as he rode. Most people were afraid that the wildness would destroy him, though it was also part of what many said made him such a great bronc rider.

Bill Linderman was talented and tough, and did his share of partying, but he was also determined to excel. He exhibited the kind of steely strength expected of a cowboy—he rode to win no matter what the circumstances, rain or shine, strong and limber or with broken bones. Riding saddle broncs and bareback horses and wrestling steers, Bill Linderman was the first man in professional rodeo to win three world championships (the bronc riding, steer wrestling, and all-around cowboy titles) out of eight in a single year, earning over $30,000 when most rodeo competitors were only earning a few thousand. After one ride he felt was not up to par, he cut the cinch of his rigging and threw it away, prepared to never ride again. He was a perfectionist, and he took his sport seriously. Of all Montana's great bronc riders, Bill Linderman was the man Bill Smith most admired.

Years later, Bill Smith remembered, "I'd only see 'em when they'd come to town, and they'd be driving cars like we'd never seen and wearing clothes like we'd never seen, and everybody'd be talking about 'em and reading about 'em, and they were the only hero-type people that we knew. We didn't have TV or anything like that; our world was pretty small." The rodeo life, the life he saw through the slats of the bleachers in the cool Montana dirt on a warm and cloudless summer day, he said, "looked like a glamorous, easy way for me to get out of the coal mines."

Linderman came out of the gate and dug his dulled spurs into his horse's shoulders. Unlike Tibbs, who was skinny and light, Linderman could not ride with grace. He rode with power. He took a firm grip on his rein and took control of the horse's head with sheer force. Watching him, it seemed entirely possible that he could single-handedly out-muscle a 1,300-pound animal. For the eight seconds of Linderman's

Bill Linderman on Ham What Am, Klamath Falls, Oregon, 1943. Photo by De-Vere Helfrich. Courtesy of the National Cowboy and Western Heritage Museum, Oklahoma City.

ride, Bill Smith was in awe. The buzzer sounded, and the crowd leapt to its feet, hollering with admiration and hometown pride.

After Linderman's ride, the rodeo was as good as over for Bill and Chuck. The next two events were the ladies' barrel racing and the bull riding, neither of which held their interest. They were trying to decide whether or not to stay for these events when the announcer called for all the children in the audience to enter the sheep chase. As parents lifted their children over the arena fence and older children climbed over on their own, a sheep was released with a red ribbon tied to its tail. The children were told to run after it and retrieve the ribbon for a prize and, after a good deal of running, tumbling, and roughhousing, one child did. The sheep returned to the safety of its pen, and the arena was reconfigured for the last events as the children made their dusty way back to their parents. As a ticket-taker kept an eye out for stray children, he noticed the boys hiding under the bleachers. Without a word, they were escorted by the ears to the main gates.

The boys rode home bareback with their hands loosely on the reins, allowing the horses to lead them over the gentle foothills, along a brief plateau with a view of the high peaks and snow, and down the other side into the valley cut by Bear Creek. The old mine shaft and outbuildings, abandoned since the underground explosion in 1943 that killed most of the town's men, stood rotting and rusting along the river. Glenn Smith had worked there, following in the footsteps of his father, Harry.

Bill's grandfather, Harry Smith, was from Cooke City. He was a wrangler, a horse trader, a miner, and a hunter. Like his father before him and his son after him, Harry led hunters to deer, elk, moose, bear, and bighorn sheep; he led fishermen to brook, rainbow, grayling, golden, and brown trout. He packed and cooked for surveyors, the men who came to map and name the territory. Jim Smith Mountain, just south of Cooke City, was named for Harry's father. When money got slim, Harry left the gold mines of Cooke City and moved two days' east over the mountains, to Red Lodge, the new coal mining mecca of the late 1880s, where he settled and made a name for himself. He was tough and surly and would always win a fight. Before long, he became known as the meanest man in town.

Glenn took after his father. He was a horseman like the rest of the boys, and he was a fighter. "Smitty" they called him. On Saturday nights he would gather with the boys after work for the locals' favorite sport: fighting the foreigners. Most of Red Lodge's residents were immigrants brought by the coal companies to America from Serbia, Croatia, Montenegro, Italy, and Scotland, and in an exhibition of racism without segregation, neighbors and co-workers regularly duked it out at the saloon in no-rules, all-out, bone-busting brawls.

In the summer of 1930, Glenn traded in some of his fighting nights for courting. On Saturday mornings he picked up Edna Thiel, the daughter of family friends Earl and Ada Thiel, at her parents' house. Glenn wore clean overalls and had lunch tucked in his saddle bags. Together, Glenn and Edna rode thirty-five miles over the mountains to the lodge dance at Beartooth Lake, a ride that took all day. When a lodge dance was held, people came from far away and sometimes stayed for several days. It was one of the only times that residents from Red Lodge and the neighboring town of Cooke City would intermingle, and it was one of the only times ladies had an excuse to wear their fancy dresses. Since Edna rode to the dance on horseback, she wore overalls. Everyone brought something to eat, and a table was spread with the refreshments. A fiddler played and a caller told the dancers what moves to make in a sing-song story. When the caller sang, "Git yo' little sagehens ready; Trot 'em out upon the floor," Glenn took Edna's arm and led her out into the crowd. The fiddler could play all night without playing one tune twice, and the caller's steady chant led the dancers' feet along: "Hands in your pockets and neck to the wall; Take a chaw of tobacco and balance all. Grab your partner by the paw; And swing 'er 'round old Arkansaw. A little more sass an' a little more gravy; Once an' a half an' swing your baby!" The dancers transformed, pairing, swinging, breaking holds, and the caller kept calling as long as the people kept dancing, often until dawn. When it was over, Glenn and Edna would tighten their cinches and ride home.

The two married when Edna was not quite eighteen, and they moved to Bearcreek, where Glenn took work in the Smith mine. Bearcreek was a small town that was built, boomed, and busted with coal. The mine tunnels ran deep under the mountains, and the cemetery sat high on a hill at the other end of town. In between, the bends of the valley followed the river; cottonwoods and scrub oak followed the water, and houses nestled in the shelter of the trees, out of way of the wind. In the years that followed, Glenn and Edna had seven children—three girls and four boys. Eileen, the oldest, was responsible and serious; Barbara was the rebel tomboy. Bill was the third child, quiet and shy. After Bill came Jim, Chuck, Diane, and Rick.

Glenn rode in amateur rodeos when he could, but the mine paid time-and-a-half on Saturdays, when most rodeos were held, and he couldn't risk losing day money or busting a leg with so many mouths to feed. After a decade of work in the coal mines, Glenn's lungs were so diseased that he could hardly breathe. Even hunting and fishing in the clean mountain air were too much for him. And as there was little work to be found in Bearcreek that did not involve strenuous physical exertion, he was soon unable to afford the four-bedroom house by the bend in the river. "He had a hard time getting a hold of things," Bill said of his father; "his drinking hindered him somewhat, and nothing ever did quite work out for him." In 1957, just before Bill entered his senior year of high school, the family moved to Wyoming. They stayed in Cody for a year and then moved to a ranch in Clark, where a benevolent family friend had agreed to let the Smiths live for free. Forty miles from town, halfway between Cody and Red Lodge, Clark was considered poor boy country. It was desolate land, enormous and unforgiving, nothing but rock and wind and a post office. The place, one old cowboy said, was "as Wild West as you could get."

The ranch house in Clark was an 1800s-era log cabin without running water or a toilet, without doors, windows, or a roof. Pigeons were nesting in each of the three big rooms. The Smiths flushed the place out and fixed it up, and they built in the front porch for the boys' bedroom. For a long time, the pigeon smell lingered. Beyond the house, the dilapidated barn, and the fence that needed mending, the land stretched east from the looming ten-thousand-foot peaks of the Beartooth Mountains. Arid flats and softly rolling hills composed a barren wash of yellow bentonite and limestone. Low, wind-blown sagebrush gave the land the appearance of coarse sandpaper; in other places the land was rubbed smooth. The horizon held nothing, save some strange wind-worn formations that looked like sandcastles washed by several tides.

Edna took a job cooking lunches at Clark Elementary School. When she came home in the afternoons, she made the cow's cream into butter, kneaded flour into bread, and cooked meat and potatoes, spaghetti, soups, and vegetables for her family. Eileen and Barbara got married and left home; Jim, Chuck, Diane, and Rick entered school in their respective grades. Chuck Swanson, whom Edna had taken in years ago when his father left and his mother began to drink, moved to Clark with the Smiths and followed Bill to Cody High School, where they enrolled for their junior and senior years, respectively.

Bill still hated school, hated being indoors, and hated learning from books things he thought would never have any practical application. When he got his diploma in 1958, he considered himself finished with formal education. His lack of desire to go to college was fine with the family because they didn't have the money to send him anyway. Eileen was the only one who had gone to college for a little while, and she was forced to quit when the money ran out. Bill knew he could find work in the coal fields, on the oil rigs, or at some other manual labor for an hourly wage, but all he wanted was to be a cowboy. There wasn't much work to be had for a cowboy in the late 1950s, and those who did find work lived hand-to-mouth. But the cowboy life was the freest way of life Bill could imagine—being out of doors, working with horses, maybe someday working his own herd on his own piece of land. At eighteen, his life was before him, as seemingly vast as the landscape.

Chapter 2
The First Go-Round

Before the advent of barbed wire fence, horsemen, or vaqueros, managed their herds of cattle in a system of open-range ranching. After the Civil War, when feral Longhorns in Texas were roaming the plains in huge herds, cattle barons hired twenty thousand itinerant soldiers, newly freed slaves, Mexicans, and drifters to drive the cattle to railheads in Kansas, Missouri, and Nebraska. They were called cow boys.

Cowboys were responsible for catching their own mounts, and they culled these—eight to twenty horses per man for a trail drive—from the wild horses that ran in the mountains and plains. After the horses were caught, they had to be tamed and trained. In those days, the practice of taming a wild horse entailed roping the animal around its neck, tying it to a post, and gradually reeling it in until a saddle could be put on the animal's back. But the horse was by no means "gentled." When a rider was seated in the saddle, the horse was untied from the post. As soon as he was let loose, the horse would "bog his head" and "boil over," doing everything in his power to unload the rider. The job of the rider was to stay in the saddle as long as possible, for a horse that knew he could throw his rider would never stop trying.

This process, so many hundreds of times repeated, accumulated a distinct vocabulary. When a horse started to buck, it hid its head and kicked the lid off, boiled over, broke in two, came apart, folded up, kettled, shot its back, slatted its sails, unwound, hopped for mama, wrinkled its spine, or warped its backbone and hallelujahed all over the lot; when the rider grabbed the saddle horn to stay aboard, he was chokin'

19

the horn, clawin' leather, grabbin' the nubbin', grabbin' the post, pullin' leather, reachin' for the apple, shakin' hands with grandma, squeezin' the biscuit, squeezin' Lizzie, huntin' leather, or demonstrating safety first; and when the horse successfully dumped a rider, the victim had as many descriptors with which to paint his picture in the dirt.

When a horse finally relented, stopped fighting, and settled down, a cowboy would say he'd gotten the horse smoothed out or ironed out. Such horses would be taught to come to a standstill when a calf was roped and to move backward or forward or sideways when asked. They would be used on the range to herd and sort cattle, mend fence, go to town, and haul hay. They would be ridden over the mountains to a Saturday night lodge dance or to go fishing on a Sunday afternoon. These trained horses were known as "broke" horses, or "broken." The process of "breaking" a horse required strength and agility, persistence, and patience. Some men had a talent for staying in the saddle long enough to get a horse ironed out and working. These men, known as "bronc busters" or "bronc peelers," were held in high regard.

The riding skills needed to stay aboard green horses, as well as the roping skills necessary for catching, doctoring, branding, and castrating cattle, became a focus of competition among the cowboys. Teams, or "outfits," of cowboys came together after the roundup to test their skills against one another, competing for petty cash or a new set of clothes. They competed in roping and tying a calf (in preparation for branding or doctoring), roping a bull by its head and feet (in preparation for castration and branding), and riding an unbroken horse. Occasionally, other events such as horse racing were added to the competition. A cowboy with a unique talent such as fancy roping or trick riding might show off for the assembled crowd.

By the 1880s the railroad extended all the way across the country, and it was no longer necessary to drive cattle north to Kansas or Nebraska. Ranchers and homesteaders fenced off the range and imported a new breed of cattle, the docile Hereford from England, which could be easily tended in a small space by a handful of men. When the Herefords got fat, they could be driven or trucked to the nearest railhead. Cattle barons kept a few cowboys on their crew to tend the cows and hired extra hands seasonally—for spring and fall roundups—when there was work to be done. Small ranches branded, castrated, and calved their own herds with the help of a few hired hands or neighbors for whom they would return the favor.

Many cowboys found themselves unemployed, and some, hungry for a meal or perhaps a bit of fame, hired on to a Wild West show. Started by the entrepreneurial Colonel William F. "Buffalo Bill" Cody in 1872, the "western melodrama" had become a popular form of entertainment from Chicago to New York, down the eastern seaboard and abroad in London. The original Buffalo Bill's Wild West and Congress of Rough Riders, otherwise known as Buffalo Bill's Wild West show, was a performance of "life on the range" featuring riflemen and rough-stock riders, fancy ropers and feather-bedecked Indians. Within three years of Buffalo Bill's first success, more than fifty shows traveled the country. Despite the travel and performance schedule, life as an actor in a western melodrama was easier than life on the range. But it was an act. In a Wild West show, the real cowboy played himself on a stage.

Meanwhile, the small contests of skill that originated on ranches grew into competitions hosted by local communities. The competitions were known as fiestas, tournaments, roundups, stampedes, and rodeos. "Rodeo" came from the Spanish *rodear*, meaning "to surround" (as in "to surround a herd of cattle or horses") or "to round up" but soon came to signify both the original meaning and the added element of competition. Most of the participants were cowboys who learned their skills on the range; some worked as ranch hands, some were ranch owners, and some were former Wild West show performers. Unlike the Wild West shows, however, rodeos charged cowboys to compete and spectators to attend; rules were laid down and prizes awarded. Elements of Buffalo Bill's performance, such as comic skits and novelty acts, were adopted to attract larger audiences. By the early 1900s the competitions drew spectators from far and wide, and several towns were hosting successful multiday events. From 1900 to 1910 annual rodeos with big prize money were held at Salinas, California;

Cheyenne, Wyoming; Calgary, Alberta; and Pendleton, Oregon. Pendleton, population 5,000, counted a crowd of 50,000 people in town for the rodeo in 1913.

As rodeos proliferated, rodeo committees formed to discuss rules of competition and conduct, and in 1929 a collective committee named itself the Rodeo Association of America (RAA). Among other organizing elements, the RAA determined a national scoring system whereby each dollar won equaled one point, and the cowboy or cowgirl with the most points at season's end could be declared the world champion in his or her event. Although by 1929 some cowboys competing in rodeos had learned their skills specifically for the performance competitions, most of the RAA's events stemmed directly from the range or "working" cowboy's skill set: team roping, calf roping, and bronc riding.

In the 1920s and 1930s a cowboy or cowgirl couldn't make a living wage from rodeo alone, but it was quickly becoming a sort of profession. Rodeo producers secured the venue, hired cowboys to gather the stock (horses, steers, calves), hired acts to perform fancy tricks and skits between the competitions, and hired announcers, pickup men, judges, secretaries, and timekeepers. The producers sold tickets to the public to cover expenses and make a profit; the cowboys paid entry fees that collectively formed the prize purse. If a cowboy won enough, it was possible to go from one rodeo to the next, sharing expenses and accommodations with friends. Some husbands and wives went down the road together, and a handful of women bronc riders traveled and performed on their own alongside the men.

Within a few years, the popularity of rodeo expanded in unexpected ways. While most small-town rodeos closed during World War II due to lack of participation, larger rodeos at home like the Cheyenne Frontier Days stayed on at the request of the War Department in the name of patriotism, and military bases abroad staged rodeos for entertainment of the troops. Troops came home as rodeo fans and participants, and by the mid-1940s rodeo attendance was second only to that of baseball. Like Babe Ruth, the cowboy was distinctly American—a perfect postwar patriotic icon. The cowboy represented freedom, independence, and justice in a land of opportunity.

Almost immediately after the war, cowboys appeared everywhere on television and the silver screen. Thirty prime-time television Westerns were made in the 1950s, and fifty-four western-themed feature films were screened in 1958 alone. In the 1958–59 television season, seven of the top ten shows were Westerns, including the top four: *Gunsmoke, Wagon Train, Have Gun Will Travel,* and *The Rifleman.* These "horse operas" presented danger and injustice to which the clean-cut cowboy hero reacted, highlighting his characteristic strength, patriotism, and masculinity. But the cowboy hero was never a rodeo star. To the contrary, rodeo cowboys were portrayed as immature, selfish, violent, and self-destructive. They were heroic only on a small scale in a specific environment for a short period of time.

U

When Bill Smith moved to Cody in 1958, the town founded by and named after Buffalo Bill was hosting a rodeo every night of the week. Glenn Smith had forbidden his boys from competing in the Cody rodeo because he was convinced that they would only get their "hind ends busted and lose a day of work on the ranch." But this was a chance Bill was willing to take. Disobeying his father, Bill went to the rodeo grounds even before the official start of the nightly summer competition. He sat on the fence and watched the local boys practice loading horses in the narrow chutes, lowering themselves down onto the horses' backs from above, and riding out into the arena.

The cowboys were mostly boys Bill knew from school. When they asked him if he wanted to ride and he said he didn't have any equipment, they quickly offered to help him out. They loaned him a saddle and helped him cinch it; they showed him how to straddle the chute and gently lower himself into the saddle. They showed him how to hold the single rope rein in one hand with his thumb in toward his chest. They told him to never touch the horse, the saddle, or the rein with his free hand—he was to keep that hand high in the sky. And they explained that in competition a cowboy's spurs must stay in contact above the point of the horse's shoulders until the first jump out of the gate is complete—what is known as "marking out"—or else he would be disqualified. After the first jump, the cowboy should move his legs with the horse as it bucks, like keeping time with a rocking horse. They might have repeated Casey Tibbs's line about how it was just falling into a rhythm, how it was just like dancing with a girl. Bill had never danced with a girl, but he thought he might do just fine. He had been riding horses all his life. He climbed over the rails and lowered himself into the saddle. The horse, quiet beneath him, seemed like any other horse in the world. Bill took the rein, planted his feet forward, and said he was ready. A man on the ground pulled the gate open, and the horse lunged out, kicked its feet in the air, and threw Bill into the dirt. This was what they called a wreck.

Determined to improve his performance, Bill returned to the arena every afternoon to practice with the boys. As soon as school let out and the official rodeo performances started, Bill introduced himself to the producer, Merle Fayles. Fayles was a generation older than Bill, a cowboy the young guys thought of as an "old-timer." As a boy in the early 1900s Fayles had run wild horses off Pryor Mountain and broke them to use on his father's ranch. He rode his first bronc alongside Bud Linderman in Red Lodge, Montana, in 1937. He was nostalgic to be sure, but when Fayles cofounded the Cody Night Rodeo, he was respectful of all the young cowboys who came to ride. He admired their courage and their self-possession, even if they were city boys. He was unusually kind, and cowboys came from all over Wyoming, Nevada, Utah, Montana, Texas, Arizona, and Colorado to get their start at the Cody rodeo. When Bill explained his situation — that he wanted to get his feet wet riding broncs but didn't have the money to pay the entry fees — Fayles hired him to run the stripping chutes, taking the saddles and rigging off the horses after they had been ridden. His salary, three dollars a night, was exactly equal to the cost of entering the rodeo as a contestant. Every night Bill worked, and every night he pinned a number onto the back of his shirt.

Like most young cowboys, Bill started off riding bareback horses with the hope that someday he would win enough money to buy a bronc saddle and be able to compete as a saddle bronc rider. Saddle bronc riding was at once elegant and dangerous, wild and refined.

And although the rodeo version of this skill lasted only a moment and was mostly about flash and style, it still had an immediate magic, an explosive energy. In Bill's eyes, it was the most prestigious event in rodeo, and more than anything it was what he wanted to do. But he knew that he had a long road ahead of him. The summer of 1958 proved that Bill wasn't nearly as good as most of the other cowboys. Moreover, he was at an immediate disadvantage in that he didn't have anyone to help him along. Unlike most of the local boys, Bill didn't come from a rodeo family. He didn't have a father or uncles or older brothers offering him advice behind the chutes. And although the local boys had been nice to him at first, Bill was still an outsider. They thought he was a novelty because he didn't cuss, drink, or chew, and even after that first summer, Bill remained quiet and shy, leaving him on the edge of the rodeo social circle.

The social aspect of rodeo meant more than just a party after the competition. Cowboys traveled together to share expenses, offered one another encouragement and advice, and helped one another prepare to ride. Most were superstitious about who helped them set their saddles and tighten their cinches—not that one guy might be out to foul the next, but some guys were luckier than others. And although his friends were often his competitors, a cowboy would always share information that could mean the difference between a mediocre ride and a winning one. One guy would say to another, "I drew that horse last week. She goes left out of the gate and turns to the left," or "He's a rank horse; keep a short rein." They shared this information with one another as soon as they had paid their entry fees, drawn their numbers, and knew which horses they would ride. Casey Tibbs once said, "When a bronc starts mixing up his tricks, you gotta know your business. If you don't, you'll either pop your gizzard or eat dirt." In other words, learn how the horse moves, not just how a horse moves in general, but how each horse—your horse—moves specifically. Does she buck in one spot, or in a series of long jumps straight ahead? Does she leap high into the air and come down on all four legs stiff as ramrods? Does she buck in circles and figure eights, or does she buck backward? Does she tend to go in a specific direction out of the chute?

Instead of always asking the other guys what one horse or another was like, Bill bought a small brown notebook to keep in his shirt pocket. After every ride he recorded the name of the horse he rode, the score he received (if any), and the animal's characteristics—not its color or conformation, but its pattern and style of bucking. A horse that bucked consistently and was easy to get in time with was known as a money horse; a rank horse was mean-spirited or difficult to ride, but if ridden for a full eight seconds would win good money. A horse that bucked on a dime stayed in one place, while a series of long jumps straight ahead was known as bucking straight away. A fence-wormer left the ground in one direction and landed in another; a weaver's feet never struck the ground in a straight line; a pioneer bucked in circles and figure eights; a sunfisher mimicked the fish that shows its belly to the sky. A horse might swap sides, or windmill, making a complete half-circle in the air; he might jackknife, clipping together the front and rear legs in the air; he might shift his gait and double-shuffle. If he bucked backward, he was crawfishing, and if he arched his back and jumped with stiff knees, he was crow-hopping. A blind bucker lost his head when ridden and bucked into and through anything. Some horses had patterns of bucking, consistently taking a few straight jumps out of the chute and then bucking on a dime or crow-hopping out of the gate and then sunfishing. Bill recorded all this, as well as how the horse behaved in the chute, if he was quiet or nervous, and any other traits particular to the beast. He made notes until he knew what he had to do on each horse.

The notebook only added to Bill's reputation for eccentricity. It wasn't long, however, before the local boys were asking him for advice on the horses they drew, since the notebook held information beyond anyone's memory. Two years after his first ride, the local boys were starting to see Bill as one of their own. After two years of eating dirt, he was finally able to ride every now and again, and he was showing more determination and fortitude than anyone had expected. An old announcer, Don Harrington, remembers seeing Bill compete in Billings in his early days. "He wasn't bad," Harrington said. "He just couldn't make the whistle."

Bill Smith and Chuck Swanson stretching their feet in the stirrups. Collection of Bill Smith.

U

On a typical night, Bill arrived at the arena toward sundown. He dug his Hyer Elites out of the trunk and pulled them on; boots always made his feet hurt, and he wore them only when he had to. He strapped dull spurs loosely to his heels. He zipped his bat wing chaps over his jeans. Behind the bucking chutes, the boys sat in their saddles, talked with one another, and stretched their feet in the stirrup leathers. The stench of the bulls blew over them. Dust settled on their hat brims, and pickup trucks gradually filled the parking lot. As the arena lights came on and the grand entry parade began, the bareback riders grabbed their rigging and headed for the chutes, where their horses were being loaded.

Bill talked softly as he set his rigging. He stroked the horse along its neck as he took the rein and drew it out over the saddle. He gripped the rein where it crossed the back of the saddle swells, pulled a piece of hair from the horse's mane, and tied it around the rope at the end of his thumb. Then he climbed over the chute gate and lowered himself into the saddle, taking up the braided rein with his left hand two fingers' width above the horsehair mark. He narrowed his eyes and clenched his teeth, revealing the muscles at the base of his jaw. He waited until he felt secure in the saddle and the horse felt steady. The announcer improvised commentary and told a joke to keep the crowd satisfied.

Bill nodded his head, and the chute opened. As the horse lunged out, Bill kicked his feet forward, turned his toes out, and planted his heels in the horse's shoulders. He lifted his right hand up and out like a young bird testing its wing. And yet . . . everything went out of focus. The fences encircling the arena, the rows of bleachers all full of people moving, sitting, cheering, these things became the blurry background of an old-fashioned photograph. The middle ground, the sand and sky, was only important insofar as it was kept in order—sand below and sky above, with the rider closer to the sky but not too much in it and connected to the ground without actually touching it. In the foreground: mouth, neck, shoulders, legs in motion. Years later, Bill cannot remember how many times it was like this—hundreds, maybe thousands—when it was all just a blur, an explosive, heart-pounding blur, before things came into focus.

One night in 1960, a city kid from Omaha showed up at the Cody Night Rodeo with very little experience of what "real" cowboys were all about. Jim Houston thought that real cowboys lived on real ranches, were quietly tough, and knew all about horses. Jim picked Bill Smith out of the crowd and introduced himself. He had decided almost immediately that Bill Smith was the real thing. Bill offered to help Jim enter the rodeo that evening, and to everyone's surprise Jim made a beautiful ride—it wasn't perfect, but it showed raw talent. Jim had not grown up breaking horses on the family ranch; he had not ridden out every morning before sunrise on a feisty horse who gave a kick or two before settling in for a day's work. And yet, when he made his first ride, the onlookers couldn't help but marvel at his remarkable control. The horse pitched, and Jim stayed square; he didn't flop to either side or flail with his arms or legs; he used both feet equally, working his body in a whole, fluid motion, as if he had a conscious command of every muscle fiber. He was able to balance his body the way a dancer balancing on one foot uses her arms as counterweights, resisting gravity with every change in position. He had a natural feeling for the timing, energy, and certainty of motion.

Merle Fayles knew world champion talent when he saw it; he had grown up watching the Lindermans, and that year's world title holder was a Cody cowboy who got his start with Fayles at the Cody rodeo. A few weeks after Jim's arrival, Fayles rigged the draw to give Bill and Jim the two most difficult horses in the lot. He wanted to give the boys a challenge, and to test his own intuition. One after the other, the boys made great efforts before they were thrown. Dusting themselves off and climbing back behind the chutes, Bill and Jim were giddy and more determined than ever. They had an unusual quantity of "want to" or "try." Later that evening, as they were leaving the arena, Fayles took them aside.

"You two have something special," he said. "You know that, don't you?"

The boys humbly mumbled their thanks.

"Go on, now," Fayles said. At his age, Fayles knew that desire could make or break a cowboy. It didn't matter who you were or where you came from: there were those with talent who made nothing of it and those with ambition who could rise and win. He knew these boys had ambition; he was sure of it. But he worried about them nonetheless. Fayles knew cowboys who had gotten discouraged after a long losing streak, took to drinking, and stopped winning altogether. He hoped that Smith and Houston knew he believed in them and that his few words of encouragement might make a difference. As he watched them toss their gear in the trunk of the car, he thought to himself,

Bill Smith on Two Bits, Cody Night Rodeo, Cody, Wyoming, 1961. Photo by Kirk Haman. Collection of Bill Smith.

"You take the spark outta these kids, and they don't amount to nothin'."

U

That same year, Bill paid his dues to the Rodeo Cowboys Association and became an official, card-carrying member, allowing him to enter and compete in any RCA-sanctioned rodeo in the country. The following June, 1961, the cowboys started talking about the summer's biggest rodeo, known as the "Daddy of Them All." One of the oldest, most famous, and most lucrative rodeos of the year, the Cheyenne Frontier Days could make or break a cowboy's summer if he was competing at the professional level. For rookies, a win in Cheyenne was usually a harbinger of professional success. It cost twenty-five dollars for a rookie to enter, and the Cody boys did what they could to get the money, which was not easy. With their twenty-five dollars in hand they went together to the Western Union. Bill was the first one in, and as soon as his money was wired, the others backed out, took their twenty-five dollars, and went home. Whether they had tricked him into entering or whether they had second thoughts at the last minute, Bill didn't know. He stood for a moment under the brown-and-yellow sign holding his entry form and the receipt of his wired money, and all his fears surfaced. He would never have knowingly entered the biggest rodeo of the year on his own with no one to go with, no way to get there, and no money to spare. "I was always dumb and naive," he said years later. But the money was wired, and he was committed to going.

"Cheyenne, Wyoming, to me was like talking about going to Rome," Bill said. "I'd never even been to Thermopolis." Thermopolis, the tiny town in north-central Wyoming on the way to Cheyenne, was less than two hours' drive out of Cody. He told his mother that he was afraid to go alone to Cheyenne and that there was no chance of him winning anyway. Edna said he might as well go, whether he had a chance of winning or not, after having spent twenty-five dollars on the entry fee. She laid a map on the kitchen table and figured the cost of gas for four hundred miles. Her old 1953 Chevy used two quarts of oil to every tank of gas, so she figured that, plus money for a motel. As she showed him on the map where he would have to go, she reassured him as best she could.

Bill left the day before the rodeo began. He drove east and south from Cody across land stubbled with sagebrush and rock. To the south, the Owl Creek Mountains glinted with snow. The road covered thirty-two miles to the town of Meeteetsee, where wavelike hills bared rough edges of teeth to the sky. Another fifty miles and the land turned red, a deep, rust red, rich with iron. Beyond Thermopolis, Bill wound through the Wind River Canyon, and on the other side the land flattened out and changed back to a dry, dirty yellow. Puckered with water drainages, it looked like a wrinkled bed sheet. Two hundred miles past

Casper, after another million yellow stitches across the land, the hills ironed out into Cheyenne. The lanes split and signs sprouted at the roadside. "I had never seen a freeway before," Bill remembered later, "and them overpasses or mousetraps or whatever, it just boggled my mind how I was going to find the right road into town." But he did, and he stopped at the first motel he saw and paid $1.25 a day through Wednesday night, giving them his last penny.

The entire town was mobbed, the streets closed off along Main Street for the parade. When Bill found the rodeo grounds, he looked around for a familiar face and found none. For a few minutes he stood still, bewildered. He felt limp and woozy. From afar he saw a tall, broad-shouldered man walking in his direction. The figure, approaching steadily, had a strong, determined, slightly bowlegged stride. He walked directly up to Bill and put his hands on his hips. The letters J-U-D-G-E were printed on a red ribbon pinned to his shirt pocket. He looked like Bill Linderman.

"Who is this guy from Clark, Wyoming?" the man said. He had a deep, growly, not particularly nice voice. Bill Smith would not have believed that the man standing before him was Bill Linderman if it hadn't been for that infamous growl. "You know," Linderman rumbled, "you and me are the only two people in the world who know where Clark, Wyoming, is?" Bill's imagination shot to Clark: rocks and a post office. He thought, "How does Bill Linderman know who I am?" This was the man who had made Red Lodge famous, who had won two world champion saddle bronc riding titles, one bareback riding title, one steer wrestling title, and two all-around cowboy world championships. And now here he was at Cheyenne, a judge. It was unclear how or why Linderman recognized Smith, a virtually unknown bronc rider from a nearly uninhabited town in Wyoming. Perhaps Linderman had seen Bill ride on one of those lucky days that he made the whistle in Cody or one of the Montana border towns where the boys sometimes drove in search of new horses to ride. Bill Smith was so nervous he couldn't say a word. The two men stood there for a moment in silence. Linderman almost smiled before he strode off, leaving Bill standing like a blade of grass, alone.

The rodeo began that afternoon, and the draw lists were posted behind the chutes. When he recovered from his shock, Bill went to the rodeo office and picked up his number, checked the lists, and consulted his notebook. He had drawn a good horse. Later, in remembering the events of that day, the specifics of the ride faded into memory; it wasn't the best ride of his life, and it wasn't the worst. It was eight seconds on a horse that bucked for all it was worth, a swirling cheer from the crowd, an uneventful dismount. In those days, the judges never announced scores, so the audience and the contestants wouldn't know which cowboys qualified for the next round until the day of the next round. And Bill was not about to go up and ask one of the judges; that just was not done. If you were a rookie, you kept your mouth shut and kept your place. He went back to his room and waited through the rest of Tuesday. Wednesday he lay in the room and did the same. He read and watched television. On the third day he went back to the arena. He had a quarter of a tank of gas and no money, and he had not eaten in a day. Edna had calculated only enough money for Bill to get to Cheyenne; he had no idea how he was going to get home.

At the rodeo grounds he found someone he knew behind the chutes, a Cody bull rider named Benny Bowen.

"I don't know how in the heck I'm gonna get home," Bill said after not much in the way of pleasantries. Benny looked confused.

"Why don't you just go get your check?"

Bill's face was blank.

"I think you won something on your first horse," Benny said, laughing a little at Bill's dumbfounded stare. "Go to that office and see."

In the office, the rodeo secretary handed Bill a check.

"I had won first, which was about $330, which was more money than I had ever seen in my whole life, and my check was right there — they gave me that check. So I went right to the bank and cashed that check, and I was rich." He got on his second horse and rode and did not wait for the results. He got in his car and started for home.

That morning in Cody, Edna was cooking breakfast with the radio on, water boiling for coffee, eggs in the pan. Chuck Swanson was still in bed. Listening carefully to the rodeo news broadcast, she hesitated a minute before raising her voice enough to reach the next room.

"Chuck! They just said that Bill Smith won the first go-round!" For a moment she thought he hadn't heard her, or perhaps that he had fallen back to sleep.

"Oh, that ain't *our* Bill Smith," he said with a lazy sort of disbelief. There was another Bill Smith on the circuit, a bronc rider from southwestern Wyoming.

But it was. Bill showed up later that day and told his mom and his youngest brother, Rick, to get in the car. He drove them downtown, directly to the optometrist. Edna had never had eyeglasses, which she needed badly, and Bill took her to buy a pair. Then he took Rick and bought him a whole new set of clothes, a full outfit "from the boots to the top." Only four years old, Rick looked like a miniature cowboy, like a toy version of his brother.

Bill had only $50 left after his purchases were made, but it was still more money than he had had before he left for Cheyenne. Three days later, a letter arrived. Enclosed were two checks for the same amount as the first, $660 in total, as prize money for the second go-round and the average of the two rounds. Wrapped separately was a first-place belt buckle. The letter informed him that he had been voted Rookie of the Year.

"That was my first success story," Bill said. "After we finished that year out at the night rodeo in Cody, and after I won the money at Cheyenne, Jim had a beautiful '56 Ford—black and white—and him and I got in that thing, and we took off."

Chapter 3

Down the Road

The 1956 Ford Fairlane had straight lines, straight fenders, and was overall a fairly straightforward car. The chrome rub strip, or "sweep spear," that swooped gracefully from fender to fender and the jazzy two-tone paint job—black on the top and white on the bottom—were designed to make the boxy car look streamlined and rakish, which it was not at all. Nor was it particularly fast. The speedometer rounded off at one hundred miles per hour, and even with overdrive on the three-speed transmission, to achieve top speed in the Fairlane was possible only by driving all out and accumulating speed slowly over many miles.

Softly suspended, the car had a cloudlike quality when cruising at more than eighty miles per hour, and as they sped along through the night, Jim Houston sometimes experienced the sensation of floating over the dark road. It felt like flying, and that was what he loved about driving fast. From the driver's seat he looked out over the five-year-old Fairlane's enormous steering wheel, across the padded dashboard, through the panoramic wrap-around windshield, over the wide, white hood and the headlights' futuristic visor shields. He watched the road for the flashing eyes of deer and antelope. He drank coffee to stay awake.

Bill slept on the Naugahyde seat beside him. He wore Hush Puppies, a cotton T-shirt, and Wranglers without a belt because a belt made his stomach hurt, especially when he was crumpled all night in the car. He never wore a cowboy hat except when he had to; he left it on its crown in the trunk with the rest of the gear and perched a trucker's cap on his short-shorn blond hair. On the seat between Bill and Jim were two books: the small, brown ledger in which Bill kept a record of his horses and a Louis L'Amour book he had read once or twice before. Bill was always reading—the current bestsellers, western dramas, historical fiction. If they checked into a motel in the middle of the night, no matter how long they had been on the road, he would switch on the light and read a few pages. At night particularly he liked the engaging stories of L'Amour; it was easy reading, the kind of thing he could take a few pages at a time. A book was Bill's tonic before sleep, even in the Fairlane.

Jim fiddled with the radio push buttons and turned the dial until he found WHO out of Des Moines, Iowa. Of all the staticky stations, WHO came in the strongest, especially at night when climate conditions allowed the AM waves to travel far. The boys knew every country and western station on the dial, and they knew that the Iowa Barn Dance Frolic featured country and western all night long. "Barn dance" radio shows like the *National Barn Dance* from WLS in Chicago and the *Grand Ole Opry* on WSM out of Nashville had become popular in the 1920s. They featured "western swing," a fusion of old cowboy songs from the plains with jazz from the north and jazz-infused Appalachian and bluegrass from the south. By the 1940s and 1950s, country music was spinning in honky-tonk jukeboxes everywhere. Its lyrics were all about love, loss, and the open road, so it came to be called "the poor man's psychiatrist." Jim and Bill were the perfect audience: a city boy from Omaha, Nebraska, looking for adventure, and a country boy determined to leave his family's poor life behind. They listened to "the Hillbilly Shakespeare" Hank Williams, Patsy Cline, Ian Tyson, Ernest Tubb, Carl Smith, Jimmy Dean, and Little Jimmy Dickens. Whoever was driving would sing along as the night breeze came through the vent-a-panes and shifted the clean, pressed shirts hanging in the back. Moths flew in the beams of the headlights and slammed against the windshield from Nebraska to Nevada, Chicago to Chickasha.

U

Bill Smith and Jim Houston, Reno, Nevada, 1966. Photo by DeVere Helfrich. Courtesy of the National Cowboy and Western Heritage Museum, Oklahoma City.

The professional rodeo season began in January and culminated in November at the Cow Palace Rodeo in San Francisco. The top fifteen cowboys in each event, determined by the amount of prize money won over the course of the season, would go to the National Finals Rodeo, and the winners of the National Finals would be the year's world champions. The cowboys who made it to the Finals had to travel constantly and win consistently; they could not afford to be hurt or to take a vacation, nor could they afford too long a losing streak.

Over the course of a year, they would drive over one hundred thousand miles. Considering all the expenses—gas, lodging, food, entry fees—Bill and Jim had to win more money than they were spending to keep going down the road. They had to think about the rodeos they entered—whether there was time to get there, whether there was real money to be won, who else might enter and be significant competition. Bigger rodeos offered bigger purses, drew the best riders and the best broncs, and often stretched over several days or weeks, affording the luxury of staying in one place for a time. But if the odds of winning were not good, especially if a cowboy drew a bad horse, it might not be worth the gas money after all. The sport was part poker, part Russian roulette—part skill, part luck, and a gamble whichever way you cut it.

Like most cowboys on the road, Bill and Jim were practically broke nearly every mile. They filled the gas tank at thirty cents a gallon and drove wherever they thought they had the best chance of winning: Casper, Rapid City, Sioux Falls, Omaha, Burwell, Sidney, Kansas City, Guymon, Albuquerque. They arrived in town and went straight to the arena, where they paid their entry fees for that night's or the next day's rodeo. They might know some other cowboys and someone's family might have a ranch with a bunkhouse nearby; if they had money, they could check into a motel. In the afternoons there were football games and cards, or they might go fishing or catch some sleep. Sometimes they would stay in town for a few weeks, and other times they were moving daily for weeks on end. Often they slept in fields or barns. Or they drove through the night. One night when they were driving west, from Nebraska to Wyoming, Bill said, "I don't like your driving, Jim, but I like the quantity of it." Jim smiled his wry smile and nodded. He would have speeded up if he could have, but his boot already had the pedal pushed to the floor. Bill stretched his legs, tipped his head back, and closed his eyes. His body was long and narrow like a colt—young, lean, awkward.

Jim was already handsome for a boy of twenty. He was tall and broad-shouldered and filled out. His square jaw and good posture accentuated his aura of strength. He had about him a certain reckless-

ness—the fearlessness of youth coupled with a naive self-assurance—
and when he struck a jaunty John Wayne pose, shoulders back and a
hand on the hip, his stature was just as confidently commanding. He
was naturally independent, determined, and outgoing. Before 1960
Jim's only exposure to bucking horses was watching a rodeo with his
aunt at the age of ten. He decided then that he wanted to ride wild
horses and could imagine no other career for himself. Perhaps he recognized in the animals a fierceness he knew in himself. Beneath Jim's
general good humor bubbled a molten temper. There seemed to be
no limit to his determination or his fury; there seemed to be no limit
to anything. When he drove he sped, when he got mad he went
berserk, when he drank he got crazy drunk. As much as he was determined, loving, and loyal, Jim Houston was wild. But when he rode a
bucking horse he was in perfect control. He was quickly addicted to
the excitement, danger, and challenge of rodeo, and his early successes spurred him on. He also loved the roving fraternity of rodeo
life. As much as he wanted to win, he also wanted to socialize, to know
people and be connected.

In many ways, Bill was Jim's opposite. At twenty years old, Bill was
six feet tall with a twenty-nine-inch waist, and he was strong in the
sinewy way men can be when they work hard without having enough
to eat. His pale blue eyes bulged slightly from his face, and he had a
gap between his two front teeth. He was a loner and carried himself
in a way that conveyed his personality: determined, quiet, serious, shy.
Bill had grown up with horses, but for all the time he spent in the saddle, he had no grace. He knew what it felt like when a horse tucked
its head and kicked its feet toward the sky, and he knew the blurred
voyage a rider took when he was tossed from a horse's back. He could
stick to a horse and stay in the saddle; but when he rode, it wasn't
pretty—he would hang on and flail his long limbs with a look of serious concentration. He never looked in control. If he won a contest,
which was rarely, he attributed it to pure luck.

"He might not have natural talent, but he's got a lot of try," was the
sort of thing said about cowboys like Bill, encapsulating a combination
of determination, stubbornness, and a positive attitude. In fact, it was

said about Bill many times. He even said it about himself. But if there was one thing Bill Smith knew for certain, it was that he did not want to wind up like his father, stuck in a coal mine or an oil field or working someone else's land. This desire fueled him, not so much for the purpose of achievement itself as for the hope of escaping his fate. And while his father, Glenn, didn't encourage him, Bill's mother and his sisters always stood steadfast in his corner. Edna had set an example throughout his life of doing what needed to be done without complaint. In her own way, she was stubborn—to take care of Glenn and seven children, to always have food on the table—and her two eldest daughters, Eileen and Barbara, were stubborn too. Looking at the Smiths, one might say stubbornness is handed down within a family, a trait of independence and defiance perpetuated out of necessity.

By the early 1960s, Glenn was unable to work at all; he was dying slowly of black lung disease. Considering his father's fate, Bill saw rodeo as his ticket to freedom. He figured that as long as he could win enough to keep going down the road, he would have no boss, no time card, no dying for half a lifetime of work underground. There would be sacrifices, he imagined, but when everything was added together, there was no other life as free as the life of the rodeo cowboy. And in this way, Bill and Jim were perfectly like-minded: they were both absolutely determined. The difference was that Bill knew he didn't have what came naturally to Jim, and there was no way to predict if hard work alone could compensate for his lack of innate talent. While Jim socialized, Bill studied his notes; while Jim caroused at the bar with the other bronc riders, Bill stayed in the car and slept or read. Jim could stay out all night and still ride well, but Bill needed every advantage of a good night's sleep and a clear head. Besides, between his father and the men from town, he had seen all the partying he needed to see. He was willing to forgo the girls and the good times to eat and sleep and dream rodeo.

U

A tire blew as they neared Cody, and the Fairlane fishtailed across the road. Jim gripped the wheel, transferred his foot to the brake, and said,

"Hold on!" The exclamation woke Bill, who kicked both his feet out under the dash, punched his right hand into the door, and slammed the thumb of his left hand into the roof as he opened his eyes. Bewildered for a moment at Jim beside him, at the still dark night through the windshield, he dropped his left hand into his right and massaged his knuckles. His feet were pressed firmly into the foot well, toes turned out. Jim chuckled as he gently slowed the car to the side of the road. "Good Lord," Jim thought to himself. "This boy's got bronc riding on his mind!"

"I was dreaming," Bill said. "I was making a picture ride! And on the rankest bronc you've ever seen. Boy she was wild! She was bucking, and I was hanging on and . . . Boy, it was pretty."

"Did you make the whistle?"

"Well, I don't know. It seems you had to go and blow a tire before I got to the whistle. But I think I would have made it." He said this last with some conviction as the car came to a stop. They fixed the flat and made it to Cody by morning, passed through town, and continued forty miles north to the Smiths' ranch in Clark. Every Sunday Bill's mother made fried chicken, and Jim hated to miss it. Edna was happy to see them, and everyone was anxious to hear how they had fared in Nebraska. As it turned out, they had both done reasonably well. In the morning they pushed southwest to Filer, Idaho.

In Filer they entered a good size competition with good money to be won and good horses to ride, but more important, Bill Linderman was registered among the contestants. Bill Smith was twenty-one years Linderman's junior and had hardly a fraction of the strength, experience, or confidence of his hero. Now here they were, both entered in the same rodeo. Of course, Linderman didn't think anything of it. The thrill was all Smith's—to be on the inside, a player right there in the dugout with the big hitters, to watch Linderman ride, not from under the bleachers, as he had done as a kid, but from behind the bucking chutes as a competitor.

Bill was jittery with excitement. That night, unable to afford a motel, he and Jim slept in their bedrolls in a racehorse barn. They woke to a steady, heavy rain, and when they arrived at the arena, it was slick with mud and dimpled with puddles. With the ground saturated and slippery, the horses were liable to slide in the chutes or to slip a hoof out in the arena and fall with their riders. The reckless horses could be dangerous in these conditions; others, more careful of their footing, would not buck as hard, costing their riders valuable points. Most horses, disliking the mud splashing on their bellies, did a skip-hop pattern across the arena, trying to stay out of the puddles. When Bill's horse was loaded and saddled and ready to go, and the other cowboys were sitting on the top rails around the chutes with the rain dripping from the brims of their hats, he paced back and forth behind the chute and imagined himself like Linderman, making an explosive, exquisite ride. His adrenaline was up, and he jumped a few times to get the blood flowing. He climbed the chute gate, straddled the anxious mare, settled into the saddle, and set his feet in the stirrups. His chaps and saddle and rope rein were wet, and steam rose from the warm animal's neck and back. Bill took a deep breath and nodded for the gate.

The chute men on the ground were slow in the mud, and their boots slipped as they pulled the gate open. The horse seized the open gate, lunged forward, slipped, and slammed into the fence. She caught Bill's right leg between her belly and the fence post, smashing it from the knee down. His foot was snugly in the stirrup and all her weight was against that leg, motionless for a moment until she regained her footing, heaved her twelve hundred pounds forward, and yanked his leg free. Still astride her, Bill held tight to the rein and tried to keep his balance as she jumped. She sunk her front feet in the mud and threw her hind legs out behind, and Bill's spine bent over the saddle's cantle, his head and shoulders whipped against her back. The boys in the "opera house," on the top rail of the arena fence, yelled, "Hold on!" And Bill said to himself, "Hold on, hold on," as he gripped the saddle with his thighs. But he knew he couldn't last. The leg pounded with pain. The mare jumped again, and he could not hold on. He snapped forward like a cresting wave, crashed over the mare's bent neck, and let go of the rein without time to think about how he might land.

The greatest risk of injury for a saddle bronc rider is not in the ride itself but in its aftermath. If a rider makes the eight-second whistle, the pickup men will help him off safely. In his flamboyant way, Casey Tibbs was known to wave the pickup men away and eject himself from the saddle, freeing his feet of the stirrups and then letting go when the horse kicked up its heels. He would sail over the horse's head and land stunningly on his feet. But every time a rider wrecks, falling from a lack of control, he runs the risk of getting a foot caught in the stirrups; he might be dragged, accidentally kicked, and inadvertently stepped on by his horse. Even if he falls clean, he risks breaking bones, especially if he lands hard on the back of his neck.

Bill's feet came free of the stirrups as he went over the mare's shoulders. The leg seared with pain again when he hit, but that was all. He had curled his body gently like a centipede when he fell. The little mare, free of her rider, danced away and stood still in the mud. They looked at each other for a moment, both of them motionless. It was cold and wet and still raining. His right leg was hot with pain, and only the adrenaline kept him conscious. He pushed himself up slowly and hobbled back to the chutes. The leg was broken. He could feel it—the narrow, outer bone of his lower leg. If he told anyone, even Jim, the word would get around. They would brand him a sissy, and they would never take him seriously. He found a quiet place beneath the bleachers, where he sat down against a rail and passed out.

When he came to, Bill limped back to the car. The pain in his leg burned when he sat or lay still and dug like daggers when he moved. That night in the racehorse barn the hay beneath the bedrolls provided little insulation or comfort. He lay awake most of the night listening to the horses in their stalls, the sounds of rustling hay and of the animals breathing. He measured his restlessness against Jim's beside him, and he was jealous that Jim could move so easily in his sleep. In the morning, as Bill threw his bedroll back in the trunk of the Fairlane, Jim couldn't help noticing the gait Bill had acquired the previous afternoon. Standard practice was to acknowledge such obvious hurts with a joke or a downplayed question. "That leg sore?" could address anything from a pulled hamstring to a compound fracture; a simple, "It'll be alright," would complete the inquiry. Bill had three horses to ride that day, and Jim knew it.

Bill had ridden with a broken leg before; he had broken one leg three times already and the other leg once. But each time he had been in the mountains, where he could sit carefully on a gentle horse and go home at a slow walk. Getting on a bucking bronc was an entirely different game, yet he knew he could not let the broken leg stop him. He had heard all the stories of cowboys who rode with broken legs and arms and ribs, and Bill Linderman was the most famous of those men. The all-around champion Jim Shoulders once said of injury in rodeo, "It's not a question of if you'll get injured, just when and how badly." To sit on the back of a wild horse like a predator, clinging to the exact spot just behind the withers where a mountain lion would sink her claws and reach around for the jugular, is asking for a fight. To make a habit of it is to court the inevitable. But while the test of bravado is in the moment of greatest risk, the test of toughness arises in the face of hardship, in the overcoming of adversity. When Jim Shoulders broke his leg in five places, his response was, "You can't stop something like this from hurtin', but you can damn well not let it bother you." That was the attitude.

In the arena, where making the whistle could earn enough points for a paycheck, the cowboys were separated from the weekend warriors, the true grit from the wannabes, the truly broke from the merely poor. As broke and determined as he was, Bill did not ride any one of his three horses that day for the full eight seconds, but he did climb the rails of the chute three times, lower himself into the saddle three times, take up his rein and nod his head and make his best effort to hold on. Three times he landed in the damp dirt of the arena, and three times he pushed himself up and limped back to the fence. And the pain stayed with him long after he was thrown from each horse, long after he limped to the car at the end of the day and told Jim the leg was busted, long after he got back to Cody and had the leg sealed in a cast for six weeks to heal. "That lesson carried me through a lot," he said. "It taught me that you can do it; you can go on if you have to, if you want to bad enough, through injuries and hurts." The hurt lodged in his memory like other hurts that had accumulated through the years. It sank from the surface to someplace deeper, to be recalled later in similar circumstances like a personal litmus test of the limits of his endurance.

For the six weeks of his convalescence, Bill felt like he was locked up in the county jail. It was hunting season, but he couldn't ride; there were chores to do on the ranch, but he couldn't walk. His father stayed close to home and drank to pass the time, to kill the pain of his emphysema, because there was nothing else to do. For six weeks Bill cursed his father and cursed the busted leg; he wiggled bits of wire down inside the cast to scratch the hot skin beneath the plaster. The cast came off just in time for the last rodeo of the season, the Grand National at the Cow Palace in San Francisco, and Jim came back to Clark to fetch Bill. Jim was looking forward to one of Edna's good home-cooked meals, but Bill was too anxious. It was mid-October, and the road through Yellowstone Park was closed for the winter; they would have to drive south and then east through Utah, and it would take them nearly twenty-four hours to get to the coast. "Let's go," Bill said as soon as he saw Jim. "Let's hit the road!"

Loading his gear in the Fairlane, Bill discovered two saddles in the trunk, plus Jim's bareback rigging. He recognized Jim's old saddle, but the new one was unfamiliar—unfamiliar except for the fact that he recognized it immediately as a "gold seal" Hamley. All the best bronc riders rode Hamley saddles, and the gold seal Hamleys were thought to be the best of the best. They had a brass medallion the size of a silver dollar stamped with the Hamley Circle "H" tacked in the fork of the saddle, directly beneath the saddle horn, under the gullet. The seal signified that the saddle had been built in the 1940s or 1950s when one of the original Hamley brothers, J.J., and his sons Lester and John, were designing and building them.

The Hamleys knew how to build a great saddle, the kind of saddle that would last a lifetime. They designed and carved their saddle trees by hand, stitched the rawhide in place, and then dried the trees naturally, in the open air, for seven days. They cut the leather that covered the trees by a precise method they learned from their father, cutting each piece of leather out of the appropriate part of the cow. Leather from the belly is supple; the flanks are thick; along the backbone is the cow's toughest skin. They placed the leather appropriately to the parts of the saddle that needed to be durable, flexible, thick, or thin according their function. Out of the left side of the cow come the stirrup leathers, the shine roll, the right skirt, and fenders; the stirrup bottoms and ground seat are cut from the cheek and the neck. The saddle is durable where it gets the most wear, supple where it needs to have the most flexibility, and able to withstand the test of time.

In 1919 the rodeo committees of Cheyenne, Pendleton, Boise, and Walla Walla met with the Hamley Saddlery Company to discuss the design of a bronc saddle. Up until that point, rodeo committees had furnished the saddles for their competitions, but from town to town, contest to contest, the gear could be different, and in some cases even dangerous. At one Oklahoma rodeo in the early 1930s, the committee furnished saddles for the cowboys that, because the stirrups were hung too far back, pitched cowboys out of the saddle with remarkable consistency, and the cowboys went on strike. When the collective committees met with the Hamley Company, they settled on "a modified Ellensburg tree [with a] slightly undercut, fourteen-inch fork and a dished, five-inch cantle, with stirrup leathers hung—and angled— forward," which they called the "Committee" saddle. Approved by the Cowboy Turtles Association in the latter 1930s, the new saddle became known as the "Association" saddle and was furnished by rodeo promoters to cowboys everywhere. A cowboy chose a saddle from the promoter's tack trailer for his contest and returned it after he rode, thus ensuring that everyone was using the same equipment. In the 1940s the Hamley Brothers adapted the saddle to incorporate a few new specifications of the Cowboy Turtles Association: the saddle horn—a range feature useful only for roping and apt, in bronc riding, to smash sternums—came off, and the stirrups were moved farther forward, so the cowboy could lean farther back in the saddle when the horse bucked. The saddle in Jim's trunk was of this vintage. It had been built in 1941, the year Bill was born, and bought by Leo Cremer, a rodeo promoter from Shawmut, Montana.

In the 1950s the Rodeo Cowboys Association stopped making promoters furnish the cowboys' gear, and Leo Cremer sold the contents of his tack trailer. A little-known bull rider named Joe Depew noticed the saddle in Leo Cremer's truck and bought it. Joe Depew reckoned he was buying a piece of memorabilia; Jerry Ambler had carved his name in the saddle's leather after he rode it to win the 1948 world champion bronc riding title. Although Joe Depew never competed in the saddle himself, he added his name in several places for good measure. Thanks to Joe's numerous signatures embedded in the leather, the cowboys called the saddle "the Joe Depew."

Bill stood by the open trunk and ran his eyes over the well-worn saddle. The cantle was short and rubbed smooth, except for the carved names "Jerry Ambler" and "Joe Depew." He called to Jim without taking his eyes off the equipment.

"Where'd you get this Hamley?"

Jim said he had bought it from Joe Depew and had since decided that it was too short for him to ride, but instead of selling it he saved it for Bill.

"It's what you need to have," Jim said. "Like all the good guys."

Bill returned to the house with his old Denver Dry Goods saddle. It was a cheap thing, but one of his younger brothers could use it. He went back to the car and looked at the Hamley again. He picked it up and admired it, ran his hand over the swells and across the seat, feeling the names carved in its flesh. It was solid, scratched up with history. He ran his finger over the gold seal.

With Jim in the passenger's seat and the Joe Depew in the trunk, Bill got behind the wheel. He punched the radio on and adjusted the dial, and across a few miles Roy Acuff sang:

Take a tip from one who's traveled:
Never start to ramblin' round.
You're liable to get the wand'rin' fever.
Never want to settle down.
Never want to settle down . . .

Chapter 4

Horses That Buck

Two years after Jack Kerouac and Neal Cassidy went on the road, and a year before John Steinbeck and Charley went in search of America, the American imagination saw freedom and possibility in the landscape of the West, on the open road. Western movies and novels were in demand, and television ratings for Westerns—from *Gunsmoke* to *Have Gun Will Travel*—were higher than almost any other genre. John F. Kennedy's presidential campaign slogan, "The New Frontier," had used popular vocabulary to recall America's heroic past in setting his goals for the future. He called the decade of the sixties "a frontier of unknown opportunities and paths, a frontier of unfulfilled hopes and threats." But for Kennedy, the new frontier was outer space. The Soviets had recently embarrassed President Eisenhower by shooting down an American U-2 spy plane, and shortly thereafter they launched the first Sputnik satellite. NASA, in its race to conquer the New Frontier in the name of democracy, had planned for a manned ballistic flight in 1960, but they could not even get a test capsule off the ground. Nevertheless, Kennedy was determined to win.

Twenty years old and unconcerned with politics at the time, Bill and Jim did not consider themselves part of Kennedy's frontier. Nor were they part of Jack Kerouac's drug-infused romp. The life they dreamed of was simple—free, self-sustaining, out-of-doors. What Kennedy said about the decade of the 1960s could have been applied to Bill's life on a personal level—"a frontier of unknown opportunities . . . of unfilled hopes and threats." But Bill's frontier was in his head. The American

Bill Smith riding bareback on Trigger, Riverside, California, 1963. Photo by Ben Allen. Courtesy of the National Cowboy and Western Heritage Museum, Oklahoma City.

West was no longer a frontier. It was conquered, parceled off, and settled. A few working cowboys still made minimal money working cows on ranches here and there, but the truth was that Bill had never been good with cows. He thought they were dumb, dirty animals, and he didn't like them. He wanted to be around horses. And the way to work with horses and, if you were a young man bent on achieving glory, to achieve some glory was not to stay home on a ranch. It was to go out and rodeo. In the decade that was brewing to become more tumultuous than any other in American history, Bill Smith was focusing his energies on a sport, an image, a historical stage, and, of course, a paycheck.

U

The Cow Palace Rodeo always lasted ten days, starting on a Friday in October and continuing through the following weekend. When it was over, everyone went home, or wherever they could hang their hat. There would not be another rodeo until the National Finals in December, and in the interim most cowboys would have to find work on the family ranch, in an oilfield, or in a coal mine until the new season started up again in January. The more money Bill and Jim won riding bucking horses, the less time they would have to spend working odd jobs to stay solvent, and the Cow Palace was the season's last fling.

In conjunction with the Grand National Rodeo, the Cow Palace boasted an exposition of the nation's finest livestock—nearly four thousand animals—and combined a horse show with the seven rodeo events. San Francisco's social set rushed to Roos/Atkins department stores to choose from the selection of Grand National fashions: silk cocktail dresses and shawls for those attending preshow dinner parties and warm suits and dresses, suedes, tweeds, and leather to "harmonize with the horsey atmosphere" for the rest of the sophisticated crowd. Meanwhile, in motels and trailers south of the city, 250 cowboys ironed their lucky shirts.

Bill and Jim arrived in San Francisco on the third Thursday of October 1961. The weather was fair and sunny. They checked into a motel that afternoon, Bill with his new saddle in hand. He took it to the room and sat in it on the floor. He tipped back and slipped his feet in the stirrups, one at a time, resting his hands on the saddle swells to anchor himself, and he could feel the difference in the new piece of equipment. All the best bronc riders rode the old Hamley saddles like this one. It had a shorter cantle and larger fenders, and the stirrups hung just slightly back of the newer models. None of these things was necessarily an advantage; a rider could lay back farther in a longer seat, smaller fenders did not get in the way as much, and forward-hanging stirrups allowed for an easier reach. But the Hamley was what the best bronc riders rode as a matter of style, status, habit, or tradition. The old guys said the old saddles were best, because that was what they were used to, and for a time everyone else followed suit. For Bill, there was an appeal to following the old tradition. The old guys like the Lindermans, the bronc riders who got their start in the thirties and forties, were to Bill what Bill was to Jim Houston, the real deal.

Bill shifted in the seat to get the feel of it. Over time, he would come to know this saddle so intimately that he would be able to find it in a pile of dozens with a blindfold around his eyes, just by touch, like all the bronc riders said they could. As he pushed the arches of his feet into the stirrups, the stirrup leathers pulled and creaked. His long legs could have benefited from tinkering with the bind straps, and he might have put blocks in the stirrup leathers, but Bill did not know the particular adjustments that could be made to such a finely crafted piece of equipment. A more experienced rider could have shown him if he knew to ask, but since he did not, he sat in the saddle the way it was, a bit too short.

On Friday Bill set the Joe Depew on a bronc for the first time. Jim helped him as usual. The Cow Palace was a massive arena, its concrete and steel roof covering nearly six acres, and the noise of the crowd was so loud it was almost distracting. Bill was nervous for the high stakes of the season's last competition, for his freshly healed leg, for the new saddle he had never ridden. But his worry was outpaced by a jittery anticipation and excited energy that took the noise of the crowd, the rush of people around him, and the nervousness of the horse in the gate below him and funneled it into a strange sense of calm. Holding the chute rails on either side of his horse and easing himself gently into the stirrups, the fact that he couldn't quite sit down in the Joe Depew didn't bother him. He nodded for the gate and was announced into the spotlights. He rode loose, as he usually did, holding tight to the rein and spurring madly. The effect was a frantic flailing, a desperate effort to hang on, a whipping of the right arm while the legs nearly locked at the knees. The short cantle forced him to almost stand in the stirrups, lifting his rear out of the seat and pushing his hips forward. It felt awkward, it looked funny, and he didn't make the whistle.

After several days of riding, Bill assumed that his difficulties staying in the saddle were because of his own lack of skill, and this was partially true. There was no question that the Hamley was a better saddle than his last one. And since he didn't have the money to purchase a properly fit saddle, it was mostly a matter of circumstance that he stuck with what he had been given. By the end of the week, he had made a few decent rides, enough to make some day money and for people to start recognizing his name. But his successes over the course of the year had been too erratic for anyone to take serious notice. Jim, on the other hand, had performed well all summer and fall. At the Cow Palace he caught the eye of Pete Crump, an established and legendary bronc rider. It was customary for established riders to pick up new, young, talent and "haul" them, paying the costs of travel, including food, gas, accommodations, and entry fees, in exchange for a large cut of the kid's winnings, which worked out to be a fairly good deal for both parties. The new kid got exposure to bigger, more lucrative competitions, as well as introductions to the inner circle of top riders; the hauler made out nicely if his kid won, and if the kid didn't win, the hauler dropped him at the next fairground. After watching Jim ride at the Cow Palace, Pete Crump offered to haul him for half his winnings. But there was a stipulation: Crump was a bronc rider and didn't want Jim for competition, so Jim had to agree to only ride bareback horses. It was a tough choice—to give up what he really loved, at least temporarily, for financial security and the possibility of fame. It was a short-term proposition and a gamble. He took it.

Bill didn't know if he would have made the same choice had it been offered, but since he didn't look like a lucky card to any winning riders, he didn't have to; no one offered to haul him. Without the company of another cowboy, traveling would be too expensive for him, and it was for that reason that almost no one went down the road alone. Toward the end of the week, when it was confirmed that Jim would travel with Pete Crump, Bill had a chat with Ned Londo, a friend from the Cody Night Rodeo. Ned was a good-natured kid, carefree and fun to be around. He was handsome, with deep brown eyes and a straight-lipped smile, but hardly arrogant. Not as wild as Jim or as stubborn as Bill, Ned was neither a social standout nor a loner. He was the kind of guy everyone liked—steady, loyal, and kind. He wore a quiet, thoughtful expression, cool and unfettered. He was raised on a ranch, and he understood the abbreviated language of cowboys. He was headed home to Las Vegas for the winter, where he was certain he could find work for the season, and he invited Bill to go along.

Ned Londo's family went back three generations in Las Vegas. In western towns in the 1960s, this was considered an old-time family. At that time, Las Vegas was a town of sixty-five thousand people; most were ranchers, and the rest were gamblers. The Las Vegas Strip was in open desert along the Los Angeles Highway, completely separated from downtown by acres of alfalfa, open field, and rangeland. Ned's grandfather, who had moved to Las Vegas from Michigan, had a barbershop on Fremont Street, across from Benny Binion's Horseshoe Hotel and Casino. On many afternoons, Ned's granddad would walk across the street to gamble at Binion's tables. He was an addicted gambler, rich one day and broke the next. Benny would loan his friends money—friends who were real friends, who he knew gambled at his joint—and Ned's granddad was one such friend. Benny would loan him money without any security. He was known to give these loans almost without thinking, saying, "Pay it when you can."

The day Ned's granddad's luck seemed spent, he fled Vegas for Lone Pine, leaving his family behind. Ned's father, the eldest of the children, asked Benny Binion for a job to support the family. Binion had a ranch three miles north and west of town on West Bonanza Street—a nice place with irrigated land, barns, and horses. Ned's father hired on there. There were no hard feelings about the money Ned's granddad might have owed Benny; they were friends, and in the scheme of things, it was really nothing. Several years passed, and Ned's father married. His children, including Ned, grew up together with the Binion children, riding horses on the Binion ranch.

Vegas in the sixties was known as "a good place if you knew the right people." It was a western town with rangeland and ranches, but it was also a town built, owned, and run by the Vegas mob. Benny Binion was a part of both worlds. He was a rancher, but he also did some business on the side. Benny had moved to Las Vegas from Dallas, where he had been a racehorse owner and a bootlegger and was wanted for murder on two separate counts. The city of Las Vegas gave him a gambling license, and he entered the casino business, keeping a relatively low profile while maintaining and growing his assets. It proved to be a good city for him, where the law, the government, the businessmen, and the mob were all in cahoots, and nothing anyone did could be too outrageous.

Benny was the type of man who remembered everyone he met, a handsome quality that could be either dangerous or delightful. To his friends and family he was kind, generous, and loyal, and to his enemies he was unforgiving. "There's no way in the world I'd harm anybody for any amount of money," he was quoted as saying. "But if anybody goes to talkin' about doin' me bodily harm, or my family bodily harm, I'm very capable, thank God, of really takin' care of 'em in a *most* artistic way." When Bill and Ned got to Vegas, Ned's father no longer worked for Benny Binion. He had bought his own ranch, and eventually he would move back to town, but all the while the families stayed friendly. The Binion girls were good friends with Ned, and he was well liked by their father. Benny thought of himself as a cowboy and a horseman, and he respected the boys who made their living by ranch or rodeo. When he opened the Horseshoe he was eager for it to be the cowboys' hotel, and he often let them stay for free and gamble on the house.

Bill and Ned only saw this side of Benny, and although they had undoubtedly heard stories of Benny's other persona and his involvement in the seedy underbelly of the city, they based their opinions of the man solely on what they had experienced to be true. "When I lived there," Bill said, "people knew me; they'd always say, 'Benny Binion's got you covered.' . . . He was real good to us." But the importance of the friendship was not lost on him. "Las Vegas was dangerous for some people, but we knew Benny," he said. It was an interesting position for such a straight-laced kid to be in, so intimate with one of the key players in the Vegas mob.

Perhaps unsurprisingly, it did not take long for Bill and Ned to find work in Las Vegas. They hired on to build the power line from Boulder Dam to California, a tough but well-paying job. They woke every morning before sunrise, around three thirty or four o'clock, and Bill cooked breakfast. Work started at six, and it was nearly an hour drive out of town. Their schedule was relentless, their routine was intimate, and nothing one saw or did escaped the other. By the end of every week, they had nothing left to say to each other. There were no stories to relate, and there was no need to articulate their exhaustion. Words became a useless expenditure of energy, and they would move through Thursday and Friday hardly speaking to each other at all.

Every Friday when they collected their checks, Ned or Bill would say to the boss, "We'll be gone rodeoing for the weekend." The boss would say, "If you're not here tomorrow morning, you're fired!" But the crew boss would take them aside and say that if they showed up Monday morning, they would be hired back. So they were fired every Friday and hired back every Monday all winter. On Saturdays they got in the car and went to any rodeo they could find, big or small, within driving range. Bill still wasn't winning very much, but he was learning. He was getting stronger from the sheer repetition of riding every weekend, and he was slowly getting a feel for the Joe Depew. He continued to take careful notes on all the horses he rode and sometimes others that he observed. On Sundays, returning home, Bill and Ned talked the entire way about the horses they rode and the rides they saw.

Toward the end of winter, Jim Houston showed up in Vegas with a broken arm. Until the arm healed, he was useless to Pete Crump and so was on his own, and because Pete hadn't let Jim ride saddle broncs all winter, he was itching to get on one, broken arm or not. Conveniently, Bill and Ned were ready to quit work on the power line and get out of town. Together, the three friends decided to drive north toward Cody and Clark. They would make up a plan on the way. Jim, of course, offered to drive.

Several hours past midnight, Ned and Bill were asleep in the car. With Jim at the wheel, the speedometer needle hovered around ninety, and they were making good time. Coming through Coalville, Utah, a squad car silently flashed its lights. Bill and Ned woke up as Jim slowed the car to a stop. They had everything they owned with them, their gear and all the money they had accumulated over the winter. Bill and Ned had spent nearly every dime they had made on entry fees to the weekend rodeos, so they did not have much to lose.

But Jim had been winning all winter without paying any expenses, and he had a good stash of cash.

"Don't say a word," he said to Bill and Ned as he watched the sheriff's image grow in the side mirror. "Just act real sad and scared. I'll handle the situation." The sheriff leaned in the window and took in the scene of the car: two bleary-eyed passengers and one with a broken arm driving, all three disheveled, cowboys. The usual discourse ensued over the assumed and determined speed of the vehicle, and the sheriff checked to see that Jim had a license. Jim insisted that they didn't have enough money to pay a fine, but the sheriff wasn't in the mood to be sweet-talked at three o'clock in the morning. He threw up his hands and ordered that they should follow him to the judge's house. Either that or they could spend the rest of the night in jail. On the way to the judge's house, Jim told Bill and Ned to cry.

The old judge came to the door in his bathrobe, disgruntled at having been woken at such a late hour, and Jim, with his arm pathetically crooked in an L-shaped cast, gave him a song and dance about how they had been working in Vegas all winter and were down on their luck. He said they had just enough money to eat and buy gas to get back to Wyoming, where they hoped to find work. Despite Jim's instructions, Bill and Ned had to bite their lips to keep from laughing at the story. The judge, feeling a bit sorry for them, asked if they could leave something in lieu of the fine and send the money along when they had some.

"I don't want to put you boys in jail," the judge said.

Bill and Ned looked to Jim with round, imploring eyes. Jim took off his boots, held them out to the judge and shrugged.

"They're the only thing I have of any value," he said, standing in his socks.

At this, Bill and Ned nearly did start to cry. The judge shook his head.

"It is not the purpose of the court to takes a man's boots off of him," he said, turning them loose. The boys broke into a fit of giggles as soon as they were back in the car, and Jim kept the speedometer clocking ninety the rest of the way to Clark.

All that spring the three stayed together. They went from Clark to Bluewater, Montana, where they visited for a time with Bill's cousins and his grandparents Earl and Ada Thiel. They played countless rounds of hearts, most of which Bill's grandmother won. Bill accused her incessantly of cheating, and she would just laugh. Having the boys around her house was welcome entertainment, and she enjoyed having them to cook for almost as much as they enjoyed her fresh bread and homemade butter. "She about foundered us on all that grand cooking," Ned said. It was a perfect respite to a long, hard winter of work and subsistence.

But they say a rodeo cowboy will always be a rodeo cowboy, and he will always want to be on the move. Jim was supposed to be careful and let his arm heal, but when Bill's cousin Bob Thiel suggested they run some wild horses from the neighboring Indian reservation into town and buck them in the frozen arena, Jim was right there with them. It was bitterly cold, the kind of Montana cold that no number of layers can keep out, and they rode until they were nearly frozen. By late spring, the arm had healed enough that Jim was ready to join Pete Crump again. Bill bought a station wagon with all the money he had, and he and Ned went back on the road as well. They slept in the car, bathed at the local fairgrounds, and tried to survive on the cheap and abundant fresh fruit sold at stands by the side of the road. By the end of June they had been south into Utah, back through Wyoming, and north into Canada. Their bellies ached from bushels of oranges topped off with shots of Pepto Bismol, and, as usual, they were hanging by a thread. For the Fourth of July 1962, Bill suggested they head to Red Lodge, where he was quite sure they could win something. It was his hometown arena, and Montana boys usually had an advantage in their home state. He knew the town and would likely know the judges, and while they tried to be impartial, there was always something about the roar of the home crowd as the gate swung open that seemed to increase the scores.

Bill registered for the saddle bronc riding and the bareback riding, giving himself the greatest possible opportunity to win. In the first rounds, he bucked off his saddle bronc and won on his bareback horse.

In the second go, he won the saddle bronc round. For his bareback round, he drew the horse called Bald Hornet. No one had ridden the bronc for a full eight seconds yet, and the other cowboys were relieved when the draw was announced to learn that someone else had the impossible horse. Others, still disgruntled with their draws, complained to friends or prefaced their rides with excuses. When Bill saw the draw with Bald Hornet's number listed next to his name, he took a deep breath and smiled. "That's just the one I wanted," he said with a cool, off-the-cuff confidence and a strange enthusiasm better suited to someone with more skill. He said it just loud enough for a few people to hear. Everyone within earshot, including Ned, was incredulous at the remark. But Bill gave no further explanation. When the time came, he got on Bald Hornet and rode him to the whistle. Everyone was amazed. It was not the most beautiful ride, but it was controlled enough for eight seconds—eight seconds that no one else had been able to master.

Bill scored thirty-nine points for his ride on Bald Hornet, a low score to be sure, but he was the only cowboy who qualified on that horse that day. And when the points for both rounds were averaged, Bill came out winning the bareback riding, coming in second in the saddle bronc riding, and winning the all-around, making the holiday his first big win in the Professional Rodeo Cowboys Association (PRCA). More important to him was the recognition that came with having been the first cowboy in nine years to successfully ride Bald Hornet. With that ride, Bill realized that his attitude had made all the difference. It was, for one thing, something he knew he could control. For another, it surprised people. Bald Hornet was a horse no one wanted, and as soon as Bill said he wanted him, everyone else took notice. Was it bravado or stupidity, or did he know something they didn't? In large part it was the bold acceptance of a challenge: the rankest horse, the horse that no one wanted, the horse that no one could ride.

Cowboy writer Will James said, "What the cowboy wants is a head-fighting, limber-back cross between greased lightning and where it hits—a horse that'll call for all the endurance, main strength, and equilibrium that cowboy's got." He added, "Nobody gets credit for riding easy in a rocking-chair." To win a rodeo, a cowboy needs a good horse, one that bucks hard and puts on a good show. A great bucking horse is strong and confident, stands quiet in the chute until the gate opens, comes out of the gate clean, and bucks consistently in an unpredictable sequence. In a later interview for the *Official Pro Rodeo Media Guide*, Bill was asked what he liked best about the sport of rodeo. "Naturally quiet and shy," the interviewer wrote, "Bill gets a lot of mileage out of very few words. When asked what he likes best in rodeo, Bill responded with what has become one of the sport's classic quotes: 'Horses that buck.'" A horse that bucked embodied independence, freedom, and fight. Rodeo, for a cowboy, was that way of life. And it was the way he won.

Instead of seeing a menace in a horse that bucked, Bill saw an opportunity. There was fire in a horse like Bald Hornet, and Bill respected that fire. A strong horse would score high for his part, and Bill just had to meet the horse halfway. He did not think like most of the others did about luck; he carried no rabbits' feet or any other sort of charms, and he did not believe that one horse was any more or less lucky than the next. Luck was in your head, like a thought; you were lucky if you thought you were and unlucky if you thought you weren't. On that day, with that ride, Bill recognized the power of his conviction. What he said he wanted was what he would get, what he said he would achieve he would achieve. In retrospect he realized it was simple. "In order to be a winner," he said, "first you have to start acting like a winner."

Chapter 5

The Bill Smith Style

Three kinds of women travel the rodeo circuit: buckle bunnies, barrel racers, and wives. Buckle bunnies hung around the circuit only in the hopes of catching a cowboy for a few minutes of attention, glamour, and excitement. As far as Bill could tell, buckle bunnies favored the bronc riders, who held the most prestige and reputedly had the least scruples, and bronc riders favored buckle bunnies because they were convenient. Cowgirls and wives were given their own sets of nicknames. Barrel racers were sometimes called barrel bitches; they were serious about their sport and didn't flounce around like the bunnies, and their quiet, no-nonsense demeanor could come across as attitude. For the wives, there were many names: back burner, second fiddle, rodeo widow.

Some cowgirls were married to cowboys, and some of these couples traveled together, but most barrel racers traveled with girlfriends or family members, people who could cater to their schedules and help them with their horses and trailers. Wives who were not competitors either traveled with their husbands or stayed home alone. They took care of the ranch, the house, the children, and the personal affairs; and they often had a job to provide a regular paycheck. Wives saw their husbands in the off-season, a few weeks in the fall and the last half of December, and whenever else they were passing through. Like any serious career undertaking, the time and energy necessary to succeed had to be taken from somewhere, usually from time spent at home. But the added stress of being out of town or on the road all the time, the risk of injury, and the notorious bad behavior of cowboys on the circuit made matters more complicated. "It's not easy being a cowboy's wife," Bill said. "They all talk about it, but that's about as true a thing as there is. A rodeo cowboy that's a true rodeo cowboy, that wife is second fiddle. You just can't excel at it without being focused."

In rodeo's early days, the options for women in rodeo had been greater. Any woman on the range west of the Mississippi in the 1880s was roping and wrangling and breaking broncs beside her parents, siblings, and spouse. In the arena she could compete in any event she chose. Between 1880 and 1942, more than 450 women had professional rodeo careers as bronc riders, ropers, and trick riders, including Marge and Alice Greenough, two women from Bill's hometown of Red Lodge. They, not their husbands, taught their sons how to ride, and their sons grew up to be world champion cowboys. But in 1929, the much-adored lady bronc rider Bonnie McCarroll was thrown and trampled in Pendleton, and a crowd of thousands watched it happen. Her death prompted the Pendleton rodeo committee to quickly cancel cowgirl rough-stock events. And while women continued to compete at the larger, independent rodeos in the East for another decade, most venues around the West followed Pendleton's lead. The Rodeo Association of America, formed in the same year as Bonnie's accident, "consistently ignored pleas that they sanction women's bronc riding and issue rules ensuring the safety of participants." Their influence and, later, the Cowboy Turtles Association's equal disinterest took a toll on women's opportunity to compete.

In the early 1940s, Gene Autry took control of the prestigious Boston and Madison Square Gardens rodeos, and it wasn't but a year before women's rough-stock events were replaced by "glamorous lady riders" carrying sponsor flags or riding in exhibition barrel or relay races. In response, a group of independent, assertive, and competitive Texas women formed the Girls Rodeo Association (GRA) in 1948. They lobbied for the relatively safe but still demanding sport of barrel racing to be sanctioned at RCA rodeos across the country, and by the 1950s barrel racing had gained some popularity. In the 1960s the GRA was lobbying furiously to get barrel racing on the bill at the National

Finals Rodeo, but by 1965 it was still not a Finals event. That year, the only way for a woman to win a gold buckle was by marriage.

U

In the hierarchy of rodeo dating, a bronc rider was the most prestigious catch for a girl. Bronc riding was the classic rodeo event—the oldest, most historical and most elemental trick of the cowboy trade. It was riskier than roping, sexier than steer wrestling, and classier than bull riding. And as such, bronc riders rarely had trouble finding a date, even if they weren't winning all that much. It was like being the quarterback of your high school football team in every city you traveled to.

Bill had never taken advantage of this stature. It hadn't even occurred to him. He had been so focused on rodeo that he didn't see much of life outside. Or he saw it but it didn't interest him. Most of the carousing that took place was in bars, where the pickings were slim, and, given the choice, Bill would always prefer to be in his room reading. If he had been interested in finding someone, it wasn't clear how he would meet her. He was on the road most of the year staying in cheap motels, and he was never in one place very long, making his prospects of developing a relationship even slimmer than his prospects of finding one. A logical choice might have been a rodeo cowgirl, but bronc riders didn't often date barrel racers; they liked to travel light, in fast little cars, not in campers with horse trailers in tow. Airline stewardesses were a better bet. If any woman wouldn't mind a here-again-there-again boyfriend, it was one who was always traveling. That, and the fact that stewardesses were pretty, made them a perfect arm piece for a bronc rider, and several of Bill's friends took up with them. The temporary aspect of it made the relationship that much more appealing for some, but how was a nice girl supposed to conceive a relationship with a man whose objective it was to always be going somewhere else?

It was all a matter of perspective. To Toni Young the road seemed romantic. A petite redhead, slim and pretty, Toni came from a nice family who had a ranch in Las Vegas, outside of town. Her father was a roper in his spare time, and she was an amateur barrel racer. She and

Ned Londo had known each other since they were children, and they had gone to school together with the Binion girls. Ned had introduced Bill to the whole group the first winter they were in Vegas, and whenever Bill and Ned were in town, they saw the girls often; Ned started courting Becky Binion, and Bill took to Toni. He liked her right away. Although he didn't know it at the time, Toni had been hearing about Bill for years. "The summer between my sophomore and junior year in high school, all the guys went up to Cody to rodeo for the summer," Toni remembered. "When they came back they said, 'We made the perfect match for you—he's a prude, he doesn't drink, doesn't smoke!' And then a year or two later, a girl moved down from Sheridan, Wyoming, and she said, 'There's a guy in Cody, Wyoming, who would be a perfect match for you.' And I said, 'Let me guess: it's Bill Smith.'"

Bill liked that Toni knew horses, and he liked that she was smart and serious. She didn't tear around and party like other girls, and she had the same strict morals and ideals that he did. She was honest and loyal, hard-working, and conservative. She was straight-laced, didn't drink or swear, and she did well in school. Toni liked Bill for similar reasons. He was tall and slim. He was a real cowboy, but he wasn't wild like most. She knew the cowboy lifestyle and how hard it could be, how so many of them ran around and drank and fought, lost their money gambling, and had their women on the side. But Bill was different, especially for a bronc rider. "He was very serious, very straighforward," she said. By the end of Bill's first winter in Vegas, he and Toni had become a couple. When he and Ned returned to Vegas in the fall of 1963, neither having done well enough over the summer to break into the top fifteen, Bill was happy to see Toni and to spend some time with her. Between the Cow Palace Rodeo and the National Finals, President Kennedy was assasinated, and the country went into a period of mourning. The National Finals Rodeo that year was quiet, but Bill and Toni went together to Los Angeles to see Jim Houston ride. It was exciting for Bill to have a pretty girl on his arm for the most important rodeo of the season and to watch his best friend compete for the championship.

There were always parties at the Finals—room parties, they called them—held in the hotel and motel rooms of the contestants in the evenings after the rodeo, and Bill and Toni went to a different party every night of the week. They spent the holidays together after the Finals, but as soon as the season started up in January 1964, Bill was on the road again full-time. As much as he liked being with Toni, there was no question what his priorities were. Meanwhile, she had her own life and her own things to do. She was enrolled at the University of Arizona in Flagstaff, and Bill's only chance to see her was on weekends. He would call to tell her where he and Ned would be rodeoing, and often she would drive to meet them. Some weekends she had her own rodeos to enter, and on such occasions, when meeting in person was logistically impossible, Bill would call her up to talk on the phone. It was a long-distance courtship most of the winter.

Aside from Bill being constantly on the road, his courtship with Toni was normal for the era—ice cream, movies, long nights talking over things they never before expressed aloud. But the more time they spent together and the more he got to know her, the less Bill could figure out what she saw in him. Not only was she smart, but she had a real future ahead of her. She would soon have a college degree and would be able to find a good job, while everything before him was uncertain. He barely made enough to support himself on the road, and there were a few times they talked about getting married when Bill had to admit that he simply didn't have the money. She knew it and didn't seem to mind.

U

In 1964 the Grand National Rodeo celebrated its twentieth year at the Cow Palace. The prize money was down to $48,625, but 284 cowboys still entered the ten-day competition. As usual, everyone arrived on Thursday, and the rodeo opened Friday. Bill rode his first horse on opening day, October 23. That same day he got his draft call. He had already had his physical and had been classified I-A ("registrant available for military service").

Bill was adamant about not going to Vietnam. He thought the war was a political mess. "I would have went if I had to, but I wouldn't have liked it," he said. "I would have never had a problem with going to the army and fighting in a war, but that thing there . . . I never blamed one person for going to Canada. I had no respect for that war at all." By the time he was called, the antiwar movement was not yet in full swing; as the war dragged on, the toll it took on aquaintances and friends must have fed Bill's disdain. But that day in October when his number came up, he had seven days to report, and he didn't want to go. The only exemption he could possibly claim was marriage, and he didn't hesitate. He still didn't have the money for a proper wedding, but the chapels in Las Vegas were cheap. "You gave them twenty-five bucks, and they furnished everything," Bill said. "They had the license; they had everything. It was a package deal. You just went in there and ten minutes later you were married. You grabbed someone off the street." And at that time, under those circumstances, people were. "Toni and I had been talking about getting married, but we hadn't set a date," Bill said. "But I was at the Cow Palace and I got my draft notice and I had to answer, so I called her up and I said, 'I got to do something or I'm going to Vietnam.' I said, 'I need to get married in the next two days,' and sure enough she said okay and saved me."

Two days later, Bill chartered a plane and flew to Las Vegas. Six-seater planes could be chartered for a small fee, and the cowboys took advantage of it when they needed to be places fast or when there was money to be won in several states at the same time. Ned, Jim, and his good friend Shawn Davis, one of the world's best bronc riders and a serious contender for the 1964 title, went with Bill. His uncle Harvey Thiel, who was living near Vegas with his wife, came to meet the wedding party. Toni's parents came from Arizona, and "Becky Binion stood up with us, did whatever it is they do," Bill said of Toni's maid of honor, "and that was about it, I guess." He didn't even tell his mother he was getting married until after the vows had been exchanged.

It wasn't exactly the way they would have done it if they had had the time. Afterward, they had a party in a motel room nearby. The next morning the chartered plane flew Bill, Ned, Jim, and Shawn back to San Francisco. They had only missed one day of the rodeo. By the end of the week, Shawn Davis and his friend Marty Wood were the

Bill Smith and Toni Young with Blue John at the Clark ranch, 1965. "Blue John was the first of my horses," Bill said. "He bucked every time you got on him." Collection of Bill Smith.

top two saddle bronc contenders going to the Finals. Jim was ranked number one of the top fifteen bareback riders and was virtually guaranteed his first world title. Bill had just missed the Finals cut. He left the Cow Palace and went back to Vegas to stay with Toni until New Year's and to wait for the new season to begin.

U

Heading into the new year, Bill and Toni had been married for nine weeks, and despite the rushed nuptials, they were in love. Toni had a naive selflessness, a factor of her youth and small-town upbringing, and of her being in love, that served them both well for that first year. Bill was also naive and in love, while at the same time singularly focused on his career. He was willing to give up anything but rodeo, which left Toni with two choices: stay at home and wait for him or go down the road with him. She had been around rodeo her whole life, and she knew going down the road wasn't exactly glamorous, but they would be together and they would be traveling. She quit her job at the bank and was looking forward to living out of Bill's 1957 Ford station wagon; she had never been away from home except to go to school in Flagstaff, and the prospect of seeing the country was exciting.

Since most rodeos lasted a couple of weeks or were separated by week-long breaks, they would often be able stay in one place long enough to get to know it. And there would be plenty of new people for Toni to meet. Being on the circuit was like being part of a big, extended family. Everyone knew one another, their wives and kids and families, and they shared places to stay, meals, drinks, and games of cards. For Bill and Toni, having had such a long-distance courtship, the idea of just being together was a thrill. For all the traveling and moving around, there would be something solid and settled between them. As they packed their things in the back of Bill's old station wagon, they were happy and resolute. Bill was, perhaps for the first time, confident. Toni had the spirit of adventure. They were giddy the way couples are when suddenly, by way of a decision and a ceremony, they belong to each other.

Bill was adamant, however, that Toni leave her horse in Las Vegas with her parents. "When we got married, I wouldn't let her barrel race," he said. "I made her get in the car and drive that car while I rodeoed and lived in a suitcase." If she had taken her horse with her, Toni could have competed in the same rodeos Bill entered. But that was exactly why bronc riders didn't get hung up with barrel racers. They slowed a guy down. Hauling a horse meant driving slow, stopping often, and spending the night where it was convenient to have a trailer. On their own, bronc riders could pile five to a car and drive ninety-five miles an hour for days and nights straight. Already, having Toni along for the ride was going to raise Bill's costs. But if she could drive through the night without having to be fresh for competition,

Bill could sleep beside her. Or if he needed to save time and fly, she could drive the car to the next destination.

Shawn Davis hitched a ride with the newlyweds from Las Vegas to Dallas. Shawn had just barely lost the 1964 world title to the Canadian bronc rider Marty Wood. Though he was the same age as Bill, Shawn had grown up bronc riding in Montana, and after a long string of high school and college championships he was ranked one of the best bronc riders in the world. Given the odds, Shawn could have considered coming in second a good year. He was doing fine financially and could afford to keep himself in the neatly pressed shirts he had monogrammed above the left pocket with his initials, "SD." But Shawn was looking for better luck in the coming year as much as Bill was. He wanted to win his first world championship.

Shawn had a sincere smile and a head of thick, dark hair. He was a Mormon, conservative and clean-cut, and a good friend of Bill's. Toni knew him well—he had flown with Bill from San Francisco to help him get married—and she was happy to have him along for the ride. When they arrived in Dallas, they set up at Shawn's family's ranch, and Bill showed Toni around town. The rodeo was to start that week, and already the town was getting geared up for the cowboys. Banners hung across the streets, and everywhere they went, people stopped Shawn to say hello and shake his hand. He wasn't even a world champion yet, but he was close. And he was the town's pride—Dallas had adopted Shawn as its own just as Cody had adopted Bill. One after another, friends and strangers reached out a hand and said the whole town of Dallas was rooting for him. He would smile and thank them earnestly. Shawn had a cool, easy confidence, not boastful but not overly shy, either. He was self-assured and genuine. Though Bill wasn't picking favorites, he was glad a guy as good as Shawn was at the top of the charts. He was a good ambassador for the sport, and, if you had to lose to someone, he was an alright guy to lose to.

Three days before the rodeo, Bill called in for his draw and was thrilled to learn his first horse was Sage Hen, one of the greatest bucking horses of all time. Sage Hen had been a rodeo horse for years, beginning her career at amateur rodeos where she gained confidence bucking off green cowboys. The more riders she threw, the more confident she became and the harder she tried to replicate the behavior. When it was clear that she bucked hard nearly every trip out of the chute, she was sent to college rodeos, military and police rodeos, and small RCA rodeos. She soon became known as a rank horse, and she started to appear only at the top-paying RCA rodeos, earning high points for anyone who could ride her. Bill had been bucked off Sage Hen before. He remembered her well.

The first night of competition was New Year's Eve 1964. Bill was more excited than he was nervous as he set the Joe Depew on Sage Hen's broad back. As he tightened the cinch around her belly, the horse was alert but quiet, seeming to feed off of Bill's energy. She was a good horse, and he knew it. As he climbed the chute gate and settled into the saddle, he had a prescient feeling that something great was about to happen. He thought for just a moment, the way time slows down in movies, that everything was in line: Shawn there at the rail, Toni watching from the stands, the crowds and the lights and the judges. Then everything disappeared but the horse, and everything beyond the dirt of the arena was diffused in a fine dust. Bill held the rein tight with his thumb up, and between his hand and his feet he could feel Sage Hen's entire body — her head straining against the rope, the muscles of her neck, her belly and four feet solidly beneath him. He was as confident that he could ride her as she was confident she could throw him.

He called for the gate. On her first jump he sunk his heels into her shoulders, and with every jump and kick his thin frame was snapped like a bedspring. The horse was taking long jumps, kicking high in the air, each trip a picture. Every second he stayed on, his excitement grew. He knew it was an incredible ride — he could feel it — so long as he could make the whistle. In the span of eight seconds, a resting man will take one breath, maybe two — in, out, in, out — and it is almost hard to imagine how an action so fast, taking as little time as to read a sentence, could be beautiful. It has to be imagined in slow motion. A photograph will sometimes capture it, and this is why they call them "picture rides"—the rides where everything comes together and looks, even for an instant, like the most natural, powerful thing in the world: man and beast moving as one. When the pictures capture it right, man and horse look like a tilted Y: the man's legs almost blending into the horse's shoulders, as if they would continue down into the forefeet, as if he is becoming a centaur. But the horse retains his neck and head, the man his legs and feet; when they move, they are clearly two distinct bodies moving in perfect opposition.

When the whistle blew, Bill was still solidly hanging on. It felt as thought he might ride her to a standstill, as some men had been known to do, however long that might take. Instead, as the pickup man rode alongside Sage Hen, Bill grabbed the man around the waist and jumped lightly to the ground. The crowd was on its feet. The judges on either side of the arena had their heads bent together. The crowd was hollering its approval. Bill walked slowly back to the rails, lingering in the dust for a moment and raising his hat to the grandstands. He was elated with the ride and energized by the cheering crowd. He knew it, they knew it, they knew he knew it. It was the best ride of the night.

The judges held up their scores, and, while Bill had never been good at math, he was amazed at the addition. His ride had earned eighty-six points, beating the second-place cowboy, who rode respectably well, by over twenty points. A score in the eighties was so remarkable it was almost unheard of, and on a tough horse like Sage Hen it was a stunning achievement. Everyone who saw that ride knew from that moment on that Bill Smith was capable of something. It wasn't an accident; he could really ride. Before that night, he was just a cowboy; but in those eight seconds, he became one to watch. The rodeo committee presented Bill with an elaborate silver tray and several checks that he took straight to the bank and redeemed for cash. Toni went downtown and bought herself a pile of new clothes. "We thought we'd never see another poor day," Bill said. The windfall would keep them afloat for some time, and the next rodeo was just down the road.

The ride on Sage Hen was a major breakthrough for Bill's confidence and his reputation. From that point on, the year unfolded in a

Bill Smith on Sage Hen at the Dallas All-Star Rodeo, 1964. Photo by Ferrell Butler. Collection of Bill Smith.

series of successes. People were even beginning to say he had style — a distinct style. They said he "floated" a horse, keeping his body very loose and relaxed and riding high out of the saddle. No one knew his saddle was too short for him, that he couldn't sit down properly in the seat; they simply said that it looked like he was floating. Some people said that he anticipated a horse's every move — that he knew horses so well he could tell what a bronc was going to do before he did it, the way a cow horse detects the slightest flicker of movement from a steer, the synapse sending the message to the muscle fiber — and that was why he could make it look so smooth and easy. But he always denied this. Nonetheless, people started to call his form "the Bill Smith style," which, years later, would be called "one of the most imitated styles in the history of the sport." He also acquired a nickname — Cody Bill, or simply Cody. "Shawn Davis hung that on me," he said of the name. "There were some kind of weird nicknames, so I was glad to get that about then, because I was low on the totem pole." Regardless, he had truly made a name for himself.

U

In the winter of 1965, two months after the ride on Sage Hen, Cody Bill was still on a winning streak. In Houston, he and Toni traded the old station wagon in for a brand new Chevy Impala, and for the first time they fought: they fought over who was going to drive. Neither one of them had ever had a new car. They traded off, Toni driving until she couldn't keep her eyes open, then Bill, and on like that until they reached Phoenix. From Phoenix they went to the spring rodeos and into the summer. Bill was on a lucky streak. He was winning consistently, and he hadn't been injured.

For most cowboys, the summer months are crucial. The Fourth of July weekend, known as Cowboy Christmas, is the densest concentration of rodeos all year. The rest of July and August have their fair share. But by the end of the summer, the number of rodeos tapers off. If a cowboy finishes the summer in the lead, there are few opportunities for him to be caught and overtaken before the Cow Palace. Bill continued to win through the summer season, and on a trip back through Cody he picked up his old friend Chuck Swanson. Bill was finally winning enough to keep himself and his friend afloat, should the need arise, but Chuck did quite well as a bronc rider and held his own. Jim Houston, who was also having an excellent year, met up with them somewhere on the road. Jim had escaped Pete Crump after winning the 1964 world championship bareback riding title, and by the middle of the summer he was on track to win the world championship again in 1965.

By the time the boys reached San Francisco in November, both Jim and Bill were safely in the top fifteen and on their way to the National Finals. Bill called his family in Cody to tell them the news. Edna immediately started making plans to get everyone down to Oklahoma City for the first two weeks in December. Headed into the

Finals, Bill was ranked one of the top five saddle bronc riders in the world. It was an extraordinary achievement in itself. After five years climbing the ranks, he was on his way to the National Finals with the one hundred most talented cowboys in the world.

Prior to the first National Finals Rodeo in 1959, the cowboy who had won the most money by the end of the year was declared the world champion. By the new rules, the top fifteen cowboys in each event (as calculated by dollars in that season, up to and including the Cow Palace Rodeo) qualified to compete at the National Finals Rodeo for the world championship titles. Competitors—whether from Mexico, Brazil, New Zealand, Australia, or Canada—had to qualify in U.S. dollars, meaning their year had to be spent competing at RCA-sanctioned rodeos in the United States and Canada. Money won at the National Finals was added to a cowboy's total yearly winnings, and the cowboy with the most money at the end of the year won the world championship title, a cash prize, and a gold belt buckle.

The idea of a world championship was created, in the words of the Rodeo Cowboys Association's board of directors, "to bring national attention to rodeo and to win for it long deserved public recognition as one of America's leading spectator sports." While RCA rodeos were usually well attended, media coverage was mediocre at best, since most sports reporters didn't know enough about rodeo to make it anything more than a spectacle. Rodeo was what one reporter called "America's greatest but least recognized and understood sport." The RCA hoped that an annual event with high stakes—a world series of rodeo—would garner the nation's interest, make superstars of its champions, gain media attention, and produce more fans.

In 1959 the RCA president and two champion cowboys presented President Eisenhower with the first ticket to the inaugural National Finals Rodeo to be held in Dallas, Texas, just after Christmas. At that event, Casey Tibbs won the world champion saddle bronc title, bringing his flamboyant and highly publicized career to even higher heights. The entire event was a success and was scheduled again there the next year. Three years later the Finals moved to Los Angeles, where it suffered from lack of community support and civic financial backing. In 1965 the new National Cowboy Hall of Fame and Western Heritage Center and the Oklahoma City Chamber of Commerce provided the sponsorship for the Finals to be held in Oklahoma City. It was the seventh and most successful year in the event's history, and the first year Bill qualified.

The ten performances of the National Finals began on the first Friday of December. The sponsors made a big deal of the event and publicized it heavily, so there were crowds and parties and a great swirl of activity. After the horrible time they had in Los Angeles, the National Finals was suddenly a well-funded, well-attended affair. Bill was "completely in awe of everything," a bit overwhelmed, and thrilled. Although he hoped to perform well, he didn't really care about winning. "I was just tickled to be there," he later said. Of course the dream of winning a world championship must have crossed his mind, but at least for that year it was impossible. Shawn Davis was far enough ahead in dollars that he was guaranteed to win the title. But that didn't make it any less exciting for the competitors or the spectators. Between the top-notch stock and the best of the best cowboys, the high-caliber nature of the Finals made it a rodeo of grand proportions. It was a pleasure to watch and a thrill to ride with the cream of the crop. And there was still serious money at stake; the difference between a fifth place finish and a fifteenth place finish could amount to several thousand dollars.

In preparation, Bill bought himself a pair of fancy buckskin chaps with cream-colored fringe, three clover leafs on each thigh, and "BILL" on the corner flap of each ankle. The entire Smith clan drove from Wyoming to Oklahoma City carrying the good wishes of the state of Wyoming with them. Just as Bill had adopted Cody as his hometown, the town of Cody considered Bill their own. His nickname practically advertised Wyoming, and he was featured in the *Cody Enterprise* every day leading up to and during the Finals.

Three days before the Finals were to begin, Bill called to find out the draw for his first horses. He had been dreaming of two particular horses, the most notorious horses on the circuit at the time, Jake and

Bill Smith on Big John at the National Finals Rodeo, 1965. Photo by DeVere Helfrich. Courtesy of the National Cowboy and Western Heritage Museum, Oklahoma City.

Big John. They were both difficult horses to ride, but Jake was actually considered a bad draw by most cowboys because he was hard to win on. He was very strong and didn't always have the same trip, and because of this Bill had a great admiration for him. Big John, on the other hand, was a horse everyone liked. He was a smooth-built, pretty blood bay Percheron, strong but gentle and easy to handle. Cowboys generally considered him a money horse. In 1962 and 1963 Big John was the Bucking Horse of the Year. The draw worked out for Bill exactly as he wanted it—Big John and Jake were to be his first two horses at the National Finals Rodeo.

Years later, Bill would distinguish relatively little between the hundreds of horses he rode over his twenty-year career, but of his first two rides at the National Finals he said, "I can remember them two horses, going to get on them two horses, how thrilled I was, trying to feel like I belonged with that elite crowd. . . . Jake, I remember like it was yesterday." Jump for jump Bill stayed with him, in every second losing his balance and then regaining it again. "He'd almost buck me off one jump, and then I'd get back in the saddle and he'd carry me a couple jumps and then almost buck me off again. Big John I rode pretty easy; I didn't have much trouble with him. But Jake, I barely rode him."

In the final tally, the cowboys competing at the 1965 Finals voted Jake the Bucking Horse of the Year, the highest award a bucking horse can win, making Bill's ride even more impressive and memorable. Jim Houston, who had suffered a hand injury in August and lost three crucial weeks of the summer season, arrived at the Finals trailing his friend and rival Paul Mayo. In the first round of the bareback riding, Jim rode High Society and retook the lead, only to be injured again aboard the legendary horse Come Apart in the second round. He placed in the next five rounds, winning the last two. In the very last, Paul Mayo bucked off High Society, leaving Jim with the world title by a margin of less than $700. Overall, Bill performed well and held his place, finishing the year fifth in the world. He had a taste of it now, and in his slow, determined way, he was going to the top.

Chapter 6

Descent

By far the greatest horse Bill ever rode, and arguably the greatest bucking horse of all time, was a big palomino gelding they called Descent. Bill first caught sight of him in 1964. "A cowboy named Leonard Lancaster rode him as a colt in the mud, and I couldn't believe my eyes—he bucked like nothing I'd ever seen," he said. The horse stood a tall sixteen hands and weighed 1,350 pounds, which was large for a horse by any standards and almost frighteningly large for a bronc. Five feet, four inches to the withers was a long way to fall, and that would be just ' from standing. Out of the chute, Descent was consistently inconsistent, which meant he didn't have a pattern—he might go any way or do anything. But he was an honest horse, never fouled a cowboy in the chute, never crow-hopped or ran out or fell back. And he *always* bucked. Over the course of his career, Bill saw Descent buck off every top bronc rider of the era. By 1966, when Bill first drew him at Nampa, Idaho, Descent was still unridden—no cowboy had stayed on his back for a full eight seconds without a disqualification.

Bill was in Chicago when the draw was announced for Nampa. "Me and Chuck Swanson, Ned Londo, bunch of us hillbillies went to Soldier Field in Chicago. Never been there in our life, got lost, went downtown, found us a motel." They lodged just north of Lake Calumet, east of Western Avenue, at a motel they found after several hours of driving in bewildering city circles. Despite the fact that it was unbearably hot and even Chicagoans wore hats to shield their faces from the July sun, the cowboys still looked and felt out of place in their pointed boots and broad-brimmed hats. The city was like a tinderbox, burning hot and embroiled in race riots, ready to ignite. Just days before the rodeo opened at Soldier Field, Dr. Martin Luther King held a civil rights rally at the stadium. "Kids like us had never heard of a race riot," Bill said. "We didn't know what they were doing. We'd never seen a black person in our life." Though this could have been true, it was unlikely for all the places they had traveled and all the things they had seen; black cowboys had been riding and working the West since the 1860s, when the first boys hired to move the Longhorns included several hundred freed slaves. But the demographic of the rural West in 1960 was mostly white, and mostly Democratic, though the political tide was starting to turn.

Everything about the city felt uncomfortable somehow, dangerous and foreboding. "You couldn't sleep at night," Bill said. "You could hear gunfire and pistols going off and sirens going all the time. One night there, about the second or third night we were there, about a block away from us there was an ungodly commotion, gunfire and sirens and ambulances. And when we woke up the next morning, it was the night that Richard Speck had killed them nurses." A block away, in a dormitory on East 100th Street, a twenty-four-year-old drifter had snuck in through the kitchen window and killed eight student nurses in what was reported to be "one of the most savage multiple murders in the history of crime." Bill was glad when the rodeo ended and they left Chicago. "I always thought that was something, right next to that Richard Speck when he killed all them nurses. I never cared to go back to Chicago," he said. "I don't like Chicago even today."

He probably would have said that about any city. Cities, he felt, were claustrophobic, harried, and confused. In part it was the physical landscape—the tall buildings, the endless grid of streets, everything steel and concrete—that made him feel hemmed in. And in part it was the people, always looking askance, watching their backs, nervous and rushing or idle and lost. People weren't made to be stacked one on top of the other like so many cardboard boxes, barely able to see the sky.

They had two days to drive from Chicago to Idaho, and Bill could still hardly sleep. There was the thrill of leaving the city behind, driving as fast as the car would carry them back to the big mountains. And there was the thrill of going forward. Bill drove the entire way just thinking about the horse he was going to ride, the greatest bucking horse he'd ever seen. "Boy, was I excited," he said. "I drove the whole way just thinking about trying to ride him 'cause nobody rode him at that time." He tried to remember all the cowboys he had seen try to ride Descent, what they looked like, and where they had gone wrong. He tried to visualize just how the horse moved, and he tried to picture himself in the saddle. No one had taught him to do this, and he hadn't read any books on the psychology of sport. The act of visualizing his ride was part instinct and part dream, and it was exactly what coaches of every sport would tell their athletes—in order to perform, the athlete must see himself in the act of performance, going through the motions perfectly, as if to set the mind in a track of action that would be played out later like a movie reel.

When they arrived in Nampa, Bill already knew he was assured a berth at the National Finals, so long as he didn't injure himself before December. The ride on Descent wouldn't have much of an effect, if any, on his standing. But there was still the desire to be the first man to ride an unridden horse, especially one as great as Descent. In the end, it was the anticipation that provided all the rush. When the horse was in the gate, his withers were just below Bill's sightlines. He was the color of the desert in flat morning light. For Bill, seeing Descent there before him in the chute was like meeting a revered person. He felt lucky just to have drawn Descent for one ride that year, just for the chance to ride him. And it might have been that that gratitude, that feeling of excitement, actually distracted him. It might have been that by the time the gate swung open and the clock started, by the time Descent took his first lunge into the arena, Bill already had too many images running in his head. It might have been that he had thought about it too much and had psyched himself out. By the fourth jump, Bill was on the ground, and he had, within seconds, joined the ranks of cowboys who had been defeated by the great dun gelding.

That year at the National Finals, Descent was voted above all other horses as the Stock of the Year, a title he would hold for the next three years running. Bill finished in fourth place, a seat higher than the year before. Marty Wood, the Canadian, won the world for the second time, taking the title back from Shawn Davis, who came in second. Jim Houston, having won it the last two years in a row, lost his bareback world champion title to Paul Mayo. Ned Londo, who had received his draft call, was stationed at Fort Sill in Oklahoma. He had qualified for the National Finals before being drafted, and the army base was only fifty miles from Oklahoma City, but he wasn't allowed off the base in the evenings to attend the rodeo. It was a strange reversal of the World War II mentality, when rodeo was considered a morale booster and was encouraged both on and off military bases for soldiers and patriots at home and abroad. Ned was horribly depressed at the prospects of missing the Finals and going off to war. Bill too was devastated. He still didn't understand the situation in Vietnam or what business the United States had being there, and he didn't want Ned to go. What he saw, or came to see, was a war where the army wouldn't let its soldiers fight and wouldn't let them win.

U

That winter, just as the world seemed to be opening up to Bill, it became more complicated. Real life, as they called it, was becoming less and less avoidable. His best friend, Ned, was going to war by no choice of his own. And his wife, Toni, was growing tired of their lifestyle. The vagabond arrangement had lost its appeal, and she wanted to have a life beyond Bill's rodeo career, which for her meant following him from place to place and watching him ride night after night. "When she tired of it, I took her to Cody and rented her a little house and left her there and never broke a stride," Bill said. "Rodeo was just all I thought about."

Toni got a job at the bank in Cody, where Bill's family had settled, but she had no other friends or connections. Bill traveled on and off with Jim Houston again, with his childhood friend Chuck Swanson, and with his brothers Chuck and Jim. Just as before, he was gone the

Bill Smith on Mexico Kid, San Antonio, Texas, 1966. Bill rode Mexico Kid twenty-two times in his career. Photo by Ferrell Butler. Collection of Bill Smith.

majority of the year, and as he rose in the ranks and got closer to the title he was increasingly preoccupied with winning. He could always come home to Toni or call her to take care of things while he was away, and over time he began to take her for granted. He thought she was happy and where she wanted to be, but he never really asked her. It was true that she was happier at the bank than she was on the road, but she was lonely. Cody wasn't her hometown, and Bill was never around. When he did swing through town, he rarely rested. He would come home toward the end of summer to spend some time riding and fishing with his friends and family, despite the fact that it was prime rodeo season, and then he would be gone again until November, between San Francisco and Oklahoma City. With a full-time job, Toni couldn't run off and vacation with Bill in the mountains on whatever day he happened to show up at home. They grew to be less friends or even lovers, since they hardly saw each other, and more like business partners, although they weren't even necessarily striving toward the same endgame.

The one time Bill always came home was between the Cow Palace and the Finals. He would come home to Cody and take work for a few weeks wherever he could find it. His brother-in-law Russell Reid, Barbara's third husband, worked in the oilfields and always helped Bill work on a rig. "I'd come home and he'd get me a job in the oilfields until I got enough money, but he never said, 'Man, you should stay here and keep working.' He always said, 'Just as soon as you can get out of here, you should get out of here.'" Russ told Bill that he was a world champion bronc rider, that he just had to keep at it and it would come. "I always remembered that," Bill said. It didn't matter much at the time that the advice of his brother-in-law conflicted with the wishes of his wife.

When Bill came home in the fall of 1966 and took a job with Russ in the oilfields, his plan was to stay just long enough to see Toni for a few days and make some money on the side. He took whatever odd jobs the crew boss had for him, and they were always the lowest-man-on-the-totem-poll kinds of jobs since he never stayed around long enough to acquire any skills. One day that fall he was out early working with Russ. "We had a rig layin' down gettin' ready to put it up," he said, "and when they're layin' down they have the blocks—which is an enormous block of tackle on cables—that they use to lift the oil pipe out of the ground; but when the rig is layin' down, it's chained up in the inside of that rig, and the cables are slack, and of course there's no strain on the cables. They're big, one-inch cables layin' slack. Well, I was up on the top doin' something, putting some winterizer on some canvas around the derrick board, and Russell was greasing up some shifts or something down there, doing whatever we do, I don't remember, and the chain broke that was holding them twenty-ton blocks up in the belly of that rig. And when the chain broke, them blocks fell; and when them blocks fell, the slack came out of them cables; and when they came tight, he had his head down, and one of them cables came and hit him just under his nose, picked him up about ten foot in the air, turned him over and he lit on one of them cross-members of that rig, broke all his ribs, tore his face all up, it looked just like you'd shot him in the face with a shotgun.

"So I was way up, maybe two hundred feet up the crown of that rig. When them cables came tight, one of them come right by my head and clipped the bill of my cap, and I didn't have any idea of what happened. I thought, 'Who in the heck was messing around with them cables when I'm up here?' And then I see all this activity scurrying around, and then I see this car take off. Well, of course you're up in the hills, and the road went kind of like a switchback about a half a mile, and I run down there, and I knew something was wrong, and I said, 'What's wrong?' and they said, 'Russell got hurt bad, and they're taking him to town.' I seen that car go, so I start running after that car, and I couldn't catch it, but I went straight down that hill, and as I went I took off that hard hat, the gloves, those coveralls, and left them behind—and as far as I know they're still there—and I caught that car, and I got in, and Russell was laying there, and he had one tooth that looked like a pumpkin seed turned sideways. He was all just raw meat and blood.

"It looked worse than it was, but it was terrible anyhow. We went to the hospital, and Russell was laid up all winter, and they lost everything they had. They had to start over. It was one of the worst sights I ever saw." Bill held Russ's head in his lap all the way to the hospital, looked him in the bloody face, and told him it wasn't so bad and everything was going to be okay. At the hospital Bill called Barbara, the sister who had beaten him up as a kid and taken care of him as an adult, to tell her what happened. Without Russ's income, Russ and Barbara would lose everything after the accident, and Bill helped them, as much as he could, until they got back on their feet. But the sight of Russ's bloody face wasn't quickly forgotten; it stayed with Bill like the smell of something burning. "That's the last time I worked in the oilfields," he said. "I started winning better after that."

U

1966 National Finals Rodeo bronc riders. (*Top row, left to right*) Winston Bruce, Ned Londo, Bill Smith, Bill Martinelli, Bobby Berger; (*middle row*) John Macbeth, Dennis Reiners, Shawn Davis, Larry Mahan, Hugh Chandless; (*bottom row*) Alvin Nelson, Jim Wise, Marty Wood, Wayne Vold, Chuck Swanson. Photo by DeVere Helfrich. Courtesy of the National Cowboy and Western Heritage Museum, Oklahoma City.

For the next two years, Bill rose in the standings one place each year. He would come into the Cow Palace with a seat at the Finals, and he would hold or increase his position through to the closing ceremonies. With the rise in position came a rise in pay, but that still amounted to only about $30,000 a year, before expenses. No matter how well he was doing after the Cow Palace, Bill still needed to work for the few weeks before the Finals. The extra money was simply a necessity. In the fall of 1967 Bill took work in the mountains, fetching the tents, supplies, and horses from a local outfitter's hunting camp in the Beartooth Mountains and bringing them back to town for the winter. He found a couple of friends at the town bar who were drunk and poor enough to agree to go with him, and the three got caught in a snowstorm. Despite the adventure, or perhaps because of it, Bill went to the National Finals stronger than ever. He placed third in the world, continuing his streak of placing one notch closer to a gold buckle every year. The following winter, no sooner had he come home from the Cow Palace and kissed Toni hello, he got a call from the same outfitter with the same job: a hunting camp had been left up and four horses were lost. If the tents weren't pulled they would be destroyed by spring, and the horses, snowbound, would starve to death.

Bill didn't have much competition for the job since most people didn't go into that region — known as the Thoroughfare — so late in the season. The snow made a hazard of the region's entrance — Deer Creek Pass — a saddle that cuts between two eleven-thousand-foot peaks near the southeast corner of Yellowstone Park; with its leeward side dropping eight hundred feet in an abrupt quarter of a mile, it was risky business to get stuck there in a storm. For a reasonable fee Bill agreed to the job. Everyone thought he was crazy, pushing his luck again as usual, but he'd managed it last year and was confident it wouldn't be a problem. He convinced Chuck Swanson to go with him by leaving out the details of the high mountain snow. While the mountains manufactured their storms, the basin kept Cody temperate and sunny, even in winter. The weather in town wasn't so bad, and Chuck thought it would be a fine ride. "He was sort of naive about it," Bill remembered years later. It was already almost the fifteenth of November.

The outfitter took Bill in a small airplane to locate the camps, and Bill made note of where everything was, knowing that the horses would move by the time he got there. He readied four of the outfitter's horses — two to pack and two to ride — and they drove out that night. Chuck and Bill unloaded the horses at a trailhead fifty miles from Cody, mounted up, and rode eleven miles west along a pack trail following Deer Creek, a tributary of the Shoshone. The trail ascended the steep terrain at an angle, scaling south along the side of the slope for half a mile. At the top of Deer Creek Pass, a foot and a half of fresh snow covered the ground, and big, wet flakes were falling steadily.

The windward side of the pass descended gradually in three curving switchbacks. They rode down easily and pushed on, twenty miles to the camp. They lit a fire with the wet wood and rested. By then, everything was wet—heavy shotgun chaps, wool coats, Scotch caps. In the cook tent they found canned fruit and vegetables, canned stews, and bread. They ate and slept. The snow fell, dampening sound, smoothing ragged ground into clean lines. In the morning they went out to find the horses. Bill and Chuck rode to the location they'd seen from the plane, but in the two days it had taken them to get there, the horses had moved. They rode out where they thought the horses might have gone and found them at the end of the day huddled together in a field of snow.

As they led the horses back to camp, the flakes were falling as big around as a quarter and their hoofprints were quickly filled. The wind, blowing east, pulled the collected snow leeward over the Absaroka's peaks and saddles. Snow formed cornices like whipped cream; when they hardened they were like waves of meringue. And where the waves crested, fissures formed from the weight of the unsupported snow. For the snow it was only a matter of time. Eventually the cornice crest would fall, slabs would slip into a waiting valley, and everything would melt into water in the spring.

On the fourth day Bill and Chuck had gathered all the horses, built fires in the tents to break them loose, and packed one tent to a horse. Each tent weighed 250 pounds wet, maybe more. They climbed between a fork of Butte Creek and switchbacked up to the pass, bucking snow and breaking trail for fifteen miles. All the time the wind never stopped blowing. At Deer Creek Pass there was five feet of snow on the level, and a lip of snow had been blown forty feet out over the pass. Bill found a shovel that had been left for foolish travelers, and he said he would shovel them a path over the pass to the other side. When Bill dismounted he was up to his armpits in snow. Chuck held the seven horses while Bill worked. The horses stood together, sheltering one another from the wind; flakes of snow caught, melted, and refroze in their manes and muzzles. Bill shoveled where he thought the trail would run, or at least a path the horses could break through. It was midday. The sky was blank and horizonless. Save for the wind, the mountain was silent. The tents, frozen to the pack saddles, had conformed to the animals' bodies where the heat rose.

Bill shoveled a path three feet wide. The snow piled on either side rose six feet high. He was out thirty or forty feet when the snow collapsed into itself with the thumping sound of two football players colliding. Then there was a moment after the sound of the fracture that was silent. Bill pitched the shovel back toward Chuck, and the snow buckled beneath him and he shot out over the cliff. The snow carried him along as it slid and tumbled over itself, rode the contours of the land, shattered, sprayed, exploded, and churned down the eighthundred-foot fall.

"All I thought about was to turn my back," he said later, "and to get my feet in the air and to kind of try to swim . . . and I shot right out over that cliff, shot out into midair, and it seemed like I was out there forever. When I hit I was still pretty well on my back, and that thing was roaring like you can't believe, just like a river in a canyon. And then when I hit, I tumbled and started tumbling, and then I got myself upright, I knew I had to stay upright, I'd heard that." With his feet downslope, as if the snow were water, as if the avalanche was a river, he made a swimming motion. Swimming, he had heard, could keep a man on the surface of an avalanche and save him from drowning. Inhalation of too much snow has the same physiological effect as drowning in water; but when the slide stops, the conditions of snow that distinguish it from water complicate matters. A deep snow burial can crush the throat and chest; burial in a mere two or three feet of snow can be inescapable.

In 1968 Bill was twenty-seven years old. He was young and strong, his slim frame solid muscle, flexible and tough. He swam the avalanche until it slowed near the bottom of the valley, and then the end of that breaking wave caught him by the feet and threw his body over like a switch. He landed face down, spread-eagle, buried. His right arm was cupped around his face, holding a small pocket of air between his hand and mouth. "It was just dark as dark could be, and it all just stopped. It was still," he remembered years later. "I was upside down just packed like cement, and I couldn't move this arm, my feet, nothing." He flexed his wrist where the pocket of air had been saved, and he pushed with that wrist, pressing his knuckles into the snow. He made enough space to maneuver his hand, enough space to flex his wrist, enough space to move something, create more leverage, push toward the surface. There was not much time, he knew, and as he worked he started running out of air. Perhaps he would suffocate before he froze. If not, his body temperature would drop, he would lose consciousness, and the rest would be a series of technicalities. When he stopped for a moment he noticed it was peaceful, and his exhaustion nearly overcame him. He was quite sure as the silence settled and each breath became more shallow that there was no way he was going to survive. He thought it would be easy to close his eyes and die. It would be warm, he thought.

"I just knew I was going to die," he said. "There was just no way out, but I thought, boy, I better keep trying here anyway; I don't want them to dig me up and see that I wasn't trying. And I started pushing. I've had many people ask me how I knew which way was up, and I don't know how I knew, I just knew." Knuckles knocked against snow in a final attempt, and a chunk of snow moved and cracked. The air came as if someone was blowing it into him. "Once I got that breath of air I knew I was going to make it. But the thing I remember most . . . I looked out that arm and out at that sky and . . . I can remember that emerald blue sky. I know that was in my imagination, but that sky was so blue." He pushed his arm free and dug himself loose.

The sky, far from any color, was thick and cloudy, and the snow was coming straight down. Unearthed, he looked around at the strewn rubble of snow. His first worry was that Chuck was stuck in it too. A hundred yards up the slide Bill saw a black spot, and he climbed toward it. He was as tired as he had ever been. As he climbed closer to the spot he could see it was just a shadow. He stopped and looked around, and just then Chuck yelled from the top and Bill hollered back as loud as he could. There was nowhere for him to go but back up the way he'd come, so he climbed for an hour until he reached the base of the cliff, at which point he could go no further. The trail was too far to the north, and above him, where the cornice had broken beneath the saddle, the face of rock and snow was unscaleable. Chuck tied some pack ropes together, clipped the pack ropes to the horses, and tossed the ropes out over the cliff. Bill tied himself into the ropes and Chuck hoisted him up. There was a path there, worn in the ground, where Chuck had run back and forth and back and forth thinking that Bill was dead.

It was getting dark by the time they had caught their breath, and to the north was their only hope, a place Bill had heard the old timers talk about: Gobbler's Knob. He didn't know exactly where it was, but it was said that going over the Knob was the way to make it out of the mountains when the snow lay into Deer Creek Pass. It was a little bump of land, not really a peak so much as a rise with a drop off one side that led to another trail. If Bill had been thinking, they wouldn't have tried the pass at all. But he was bulletproof, immortal. Gobbler's Knob was a safety precaution, a last resort.

With the packhorses between them, Chuck led off. They found the Knob without too much trouble, but once there Chuck argued against going. It was a ten-foot sheer drop. After watching his friend nearly die, Chuck was terrified. Bill said there was no alternative, save to stay put, sleep, and wait until spring. He pushed the packhorses over the drop; Chuck's horse went off and Bill's horse followed, landing uninjured, and Bill and Chuck scrambled down after the horses.

They rode out along Deer Creek to the road, dipping below timberline. Two feet of snow hid the trail, dusk was falling, and Chuck, in the lead, said he no longer knew where they were. Bill rode up to take the lead. He reached for the rope of the packhorse Chuck was trailing and, as his gloved hand closed around the length of braided cotton, he realized all four knuckles were broken, all four knuckles of the hand that had broken him free.

They rode out eleven miles in silence. When they reached the trucks parked at the trailhead, they loaded the horses and ran the engines to warm them. They climbed in the cabs and tried to warm themselves without falling asleep, but by then the heat barely mattered; they were numb with exhaustion, practically unable to feel. They drove into town fifty dark, quiet miles. And all during that dark ride to town, death seemed still close. In one account of avalanche survival, a man who appeared fine when he was rescued died of shock four days later in the hospital, his body curled in bed in the same position as he was found in the snow.

It was midnight by the time they arrived home. Town was in an uproar; they had been searching for two or three days already, and they wanted to hear the story, but Bill was tired and cold to the core, too tired to talk or eat or think of anything. Toni ran him a hot bath while he took off his clothes, dropped the clothes in a pile on the floor, stepped one foot and then the other into the hot water. In minutes his torn flesh leaked blood, and the bathwater turned red. He called to Toni who came to him, helped him lift his body out of the bath and into bed where, for five days, he heard nothing but the roar of snow. "I said, 'Get me in that bed and I'll sleep for a month.' And I got in that bed, and every time I closed my eyes for four or five days I would hear that roar. I didn't sleep a wink for four or five days. Tell that story I'd break out in a cold sweat for years." For his part, Chuck was furious with Bill for having put them both in what he considered a foolish position, and he wouldn't speak to Bill of the incident for many years afterward.

"If you could see where it was, you would be amazed," Bill said. "That's one time when I knew for sure that I was going to die. That's why I'm ready, when it comes my time to die, I'm not going to be too terrified of it. It's not going to be that bad. Seemed like when I was in there, that would have been an easy thing to do, just close my eyes and give up and kind of a warm feeling would come. I just had to fight like heck."

Chapter 7

Winning the World

Throughout Bill Smith's life, good did come with bad, strokes of luck often touched elements of disaster, and the year he called his "magic year" was no different. Bill came out of the 1968 National Finals in second place, so close to a world championship it made his teeth hurt. The same cast of characters was at the top of the charts coming into the new season: Marty Wood and Shawn Davis, three-time all-around world champion Larry Mahan, and a relative newcomer, Bobby Berger of Halstead, Kansas, was having a great start. In Denver at the first rodeo of 1969, Bill drew Descent for the second time in his career, and Descent bucked him off so hard that Bill broke two ribs. He went from having won the Denver rodeo in January 1968 to not winning a dime in 1969. At Fort Worth he picked up $850, but he still trailed the top five. Then, in the space of four weeks, he earned $2,685 for a first-place win in Houston, $546 for second place in Tucson, and $1,513 for a win in San Antonio. After $5,600 of winnings in four weeks he was, for a moment, in the lead.

The next several months were consistent but slow. Bill rode well, but he wasn't winning much. Shawn moved back into the top spot. For the past five years, Shawn and Marty had traded the title back and forth, while Bill had moved up the ranks steadily, finishing fifth, fourth, third, and second. Bill's grandmother Ada Theil said she wished Marty or Shawn would just break an arm and give someone else a shot at winning the world. She said it with a sense of humor and certainly didn't wish them any harm; after all, they were Bill's friends.

But by some stroke of fate, Marty did break his arm. And then that May, in Thompson Falls, Montana, a bronc came over backward on Shawn and broke his back. At least one surgeon predicted that he would never be able to ride even a gentle horse again.

Shawn went home to Dallas for surgery while the rest of the cowboys went to Lehi, Utah. Behind the chutes Bill sat with the other top riders talking about how Shawn getting hurt would affect the world championship. Larry Mahan and Bobby Berger were two of the talkers and two of the top contenders, and they rattled off names of guys they thought might have a chance. Bill, ranked fourth or fifth, expected to hear his name, but it was never mentioned.

At Lehi, Bill had drawn a second-rate horse and, hoping for something better at the next location, he called ahead to Reno, Nevada, to hear the draw. He didn't know the horse he'd drawn at Reno, but his friend Jack Sparrick had ridden the horse recently. Bill asked Jack how the horse was, and Jack said he was bad. The horse had stopped stone still with Jack, and Jack got a re-ride. Bill deflated. With two bad horses in a row there was little chance he would catch the front-runners; what little standing he had would drop even further and be harder to recover. With a bad horse at Reno it was almost not worth it to go. There was no sense spending money on entry fees when there was no hope of winning. But then, recalling his ride on Bald Hornet in 1962, Bill thought that maybe turning those horses out wasn't the best idea. He was already there in Lehi, so it wouldn't cost him anything to ride the first of his bad draws.

Bill got on the horse at Lehi that wasn't supposed to be any good, and the little horse bucked, and he won first place. "The heck with it," he said, "I'm going to go try to get on that horse at Reno. Maybe he'll stop and I'll get a re-ride and my re-ride will be good." And lo and behold, Bill got on the horse at Reno and the horse bucked, and Bill won first place. He won $918. From Reno he went to Calgary and from Calgary to the Fourth of July rodeos. He chartered a plane with some of the boys, including his brother Jim, and flew from Calgary to Mobridge, South Dakota. From South Dakota they flew to Montana and rode in Livingston, Red Lodge, and Cody, Wyoming, all in one day. Then they

Bill Smith on RR Bronc, Calgary, Alberta, 1969. Photo by Fred Kobsted. Collection of Bill Smith.

flew back to Mobridge, on to LeMars, Iowa, and back to Calgary in the space of five days. He placed first at Red Lodge and Mobridge, second at Calgary and LeMars. In the middle of July he went to Salinas, California, and won second. He won first at Salt Lake and came back to Wyoming for the Cheyenne Frontier Days and placed second. In thirty days he had won $7,000, putting him in the lead by over $4,000, and three weeks earlier no one even thought he was entered.

Considering how quickly things had changed, Bill could have been worried about losing his lead, but the summer rodeos were where the big money was won, and the summer was nearly over. That year, 1969, was never a race after July; Bill never lost his lead and never looked back. By November he was still $5,000 in the lead, and even a disastrous showing at the Cow Palace in San Francisco was not enough to throw him off track: he won only $203, while the all-around world champion cowboy Larry Mahan took first for $1,217. But the

Jim Smith on Crazy One at the National Finals Rodeo, 1969. Three of the seven Smith children—Bill, Jim, and Rick—competed at the National Finals Rodeo. Photo by Ferrell Butler. Collection of Bill Smith.

maximum possible winnings at the National Finals in a single event was $4,325, and Bill was still $3,847 ahead. Mahan could win only if he placed first on each of his nine broncs and Bill did not score on a single one. Jim Smith was also assured a spot at the Finals that year, and the brothers traveled together to Oklahoma City with a good deal of excitement.

On December 8, two days into competition at the National Finals Rodeo, Bill received a telegram from Western Union. It read, "The entire town of Cody is behind you—Good luck in the 1969 National Finals." He had become, like Shawn Davis in Dallas, a town hero. Cafés posted the newspaper clippings by their registers, and locals followed his winnings with relish. By the time he received the telegram from town, he didn't need much luck. The Finals were practically in the

Glenn and Edna Smith at Bill's house in Cody, on the way to the town's dinner held in Bill's honor, 1969. The plates on the mantle (*left and right*) Bill won at Nampa; the plate in the center Bill won in Dallas on Sage Hen in 1964. Collection of Bill Smith.

bag. He rode well in every round, and six days later the championship was won. At the closing ceremony he was awarded a coveted gold buckle studded with gemstones, which he immediately gave to his mother. Having received it earned him the privilege of belonging to the Gold Buckle Club, the group of cowboys who had won a world championship title, which was like a fraternity of the best of the best.

He also received a check for his winnings in Oklahoma City and various other sponsor prizes and gifts. More telegrams and letters arrived from friends and family. Senator Dale W. McGee sent his congratulations, and the National Cowboy Hall of Fame and Winchester-Western sent a note with a cowboy commemorative 30-caliber 1894 model carbine, "as a token of our high regard."

The town of Cody named December 29, 1969, "Bill Smith Day" and celebrated with a banquet at the Cody Auditorium. By his tenth year as a professional rodeo cowboy, Bill had cumulatively won over $90,000. In 1969, with winnings totaling $23,642, he was the best bronc rider in the world. On that day, he joined the ranks of Bill Linderman, Casey Tibbs, and his friends Marty Wood and Shawn Davis. He was twenty-eight years old.

U

The year after his first world, Bill took it easy and stayed closer to home. He needed the time to relax after all the hectic traveling of the past year, and he needed to spend some time with Toni. He had hardly seen her in the last twelve months. She still had her job at the bank, and she had made many friends in Cody, but she was beginning to wonder whether being married to someone who was never around was worth the effort. She still loved Bill, and she wanted him to be home more often, but Bill was not the type to keep still. Even when he decided to spend more time at home, he was rarely there. In the late sixties, he had taken over the Yellow Creek Camp Outfitters, a hunting camp owned by a friend, and during the 1970 hunting season he spent more time guiding trips in the Beartooth Mountains than he did rodeoing. In the summer, he hired out and gathered cattle with his brothers, and every so often he would go to a rodeo.

Despite not riding much, or perhaps because of it, he rode well at the few rodeos he attended that year, except for a bad wreck in Salt Lake that hurt two vertebrae in his lower back and damaged his tailbone. Instead of going to the hospital, he continued on to Cheyenne and won. With only twenty-eight rodeo appearances that year, roughly half of his usual total, he still managed to enter the National Finals in tenth place. But it was a let-down to be at the Finals and not even stand a chance of winning. The following January he put his energy back into riding full-time. The year of rest had done his mind and body good, and he was fresh for the new season.

In Denver at the first big rodeo of the 1971 season, Bill watched a kid make a beautiful bareback ride on a horse called Smokey. The horse was a notoriously difficult one, and the kid rode him perfectly, except he failed to spur the horse out and was disqualified. Bill turned to the cowboys next to him and said, "Who is that guy? That's the best bareback rider I've ever seen, and I traveled with Jim Houston all those years and Jim Houston was the best bareback rider in the world. This guy looks as good or better than Jim!" Jim Houston had gotten too big to be a bareback rider and had moved on to steer wrestling. The cowboys on the rail said the kid was Joe Alexander from Cora, Wyoming.

As soon as they said it, Bill remembered having met the kid once before. In 1968 Bill had been invited to a matched bronc riding event in Sheridan, Wyoming, with Shawn Davis. The two bronc riders were to each ride three horses, winner take all. Shawn was the world champion that year and was popular wherever he went. Shawn had also been invited to this matched bronc riding event at Sheridan two or three times already, and he had won it each time, so everyone knew him and was happy to see him. Bill didn't know anyone in Sheridan, and no one really knew him yet, which was surprising since Sheridan isn't far from Cody. But he hadn't yet won his first championship, and Shawn had already won two. As the two bronc riders got ready for the rodeo, Shawn's chute was crowded with a cluster of friends and hangers-on, and Bill was by himself. And then a neatly dressed kid in a nice hat appeared by the side of Bill's chute. The kid asked Bill if he needed some help getting ready, and Bill said he did, and the kid introduced himself as Joe Alexander from Cora, Wyoming. He had won the national intercollegiate title in 1966.

When Bill noticed Joe again in 1971 the kid was a professional rodeo cowboy, but he wasn't making any money, because he kept disqualifying himself. Bill didn't say anything to the kid in Denver, but he saw him again in Fort Worth and San Antonio. The kid's losing streak had continued, and before the season had really even begun he was almost out of cash. Toward the end of the rodeo in San Antonio, Bill got a call in his motel room. The kid admitted he wasn't having any luck and was wondering if he could travel with Bill. Bill said he was headed to Tucson next and, so long as that suited Joe, he was welcome to come along. That spring and into the summer they traveled together. It was a good partnership, like the one Bill had with Jim Houston, because they rode in different events and could always help each other behind the chutes. As Bill got to know the kid better and watched him ride, he tried to help Joe learn to spur his horses out. The kid was so much better than everybody else that, so long as he didn't disqualify, he met with great success. But the successful rides were few and far between, and Joe was frustrated. His frustration kept him from breaking his habit, and almost from riding entirely.

For the Fourth of July rodeos Bill chartered a plane for five days. Everyone was tired by that time, but the Fourth is when a cowboy can make or break his year; Bill had already proved that to himself in 1969. Every year between the first and the fifth or sixth of July he would enter ten or twelve rodeos and fly back and forth from one to the other. "We'd have it scheduled, and you'd go without meals and without sleep and no shaves or might not even get to bed, but you'd go and get on at all them rodeos," he said. A week before the 1971 whirlwind started, Joe and Bill called from Bill's house in Cody to find out when they were up and what they had drawn at all the rodeos they'd entered. Joe didn't like what he drew. He was tired, downcast, and fed up. He said, "I'm turning 'em all out." But Bill couldn't stand to let the kid quit; he had so much talent, more than Bill had ever seen in anyone. "I just lit into him and bullied him and shamed him and flat drug him and got him on that airplane, and I think he might have won all but one of them rodeos, might have won all of them, I don't remember. But when he came out of that Fourth of July, he was far ahead of anybody else for the title, and never looked back."

In the fall, Bill was at the top of his game when he drew Descent in Nampa, Idaho, again. Since 1966 both he and the horse had grown

1971 National Finals Rodeo bronc riders. (*Top row, left to right*) Tommy Tate, Doug Brown, John Holman, Ralph Maynard, Kenny McClean; (*middle row*) Larry Jourdan, John Macbeth, Bill Nelson, Bobby Berger, Dennis Reiners; (*bottom row*) Bill Smith, Shawn Davis, J. C. Bonine, Bill Martinelli, Mel Hyland. Photo by Ferrell Butler. Courtesy of the National Cowboy and Western Heritage Museum.

tougher and wiser. When they met in 1971 they were equals, both of them world champions. For Bill this was the only honest kind of competition—when the horse had every opportunity and bucked hard in top form. But Bill's top form had as much to do with his confidence as it did to do with his talent. By 1971 Descent had been ridden to the whistle. And by the time they met in Nampa, Bill was so far ahead in the standings that he was for the second time in three years ranked the best bronc rider in the world. "How I rode him I'll never know," he said of what he considered the best ride of his career. "It was just a nip and tuck thing where every jump I might not make it, and every jump

I did make it. He took a little bit of the rein away from me every jump, and I was hanging on for all I was worth. I never did hear the whistle blow; I rode him as far as I could, and he finally threw me off." Only later did he learn he had made the whistle. It was the greatest ride on the greatest bucking horse he'd ever known.

By the end of July, Bill was virtually assured of winning his second world title, and he did. This time, he kept the gold buckle for himself. It was a buckle he earned, and, although people had continued to support him and help him along they way, he didn't feel he owed it to anyone but himself. Joe Alexander won his first world title that year, the first of five straight years that he would win and for which he would come to be known as "Alexander the Great," and he credited Bill for his year's success. From that point on, Bill and Joe traveled in style. Joe continued to ride bareback horses, and Bill rode saddle broncs, and they both won. They were able to stay in motels, charter planes, and eat regularly.

U

Since Earl Thode was declared the champion saddle bronc rider of 1929, only nine cowboys have won the championship more than twice. Four of them—Clint Johnson, Brad Gjermundson, Billy Etbauer, and Dan Mortensen—have won their titles since 1980, a time in which corporate sponsorships have made going down the road easier on the wallet and advances in safety and technology have made riding easier on the body. Before 1980, only five men had managed it.

After his win in 1971, Bill repeated the pattern of the previous two years, taking a rest year in 1972, trying to stay home more and rodeo less. But Toni saw the pattern too, and she knew that Bill was only thirty years old and had several more years of rodeo left in him. Unless she said something, he would be on the road like this maybe another ten years. Or worse, he would ride too long and be injured. They still had no children, even though Bill loved kids, and if they did he would never be around to see them. From Toni's perspective, it was simple: "I didn't think rodeo was a life for kids, dragging them around. It was too hard on everybody."

"I should have spent a lot more time at home," Bill said later, not just of that year but of all the years he was married to her. "Toni was a wonderful girl. She was just alone all the time. I was just never there, and I was hard-headed and ignorant and couldn't see it. And she just wanted something for herself. She got tired of being Bill Smith's wife. She wanted to be herself, and she had a lot on the ball, and I couldn't understand it. She tried to tell me. And I couldn't hear it."

Although he loved her, there was no part of him that wanted to compromise his passion or his lifestyle, so what he heard was filtered through a sieve of his own desires. Toni wanted to go back to school and get a four-year degree, and Bill didn't think she needed to; Toni wanted to cut her hair short, and Bill wanted her to keep her hair long, like a lady; Toni wanted to have her own life, and Bill wanted her to drive the car and wait for him. It was as if he was watching a movie in 3-D, his paper and plastic glasses tinted red and green, and he could not explain to her the dimension beyond what she could see with only the naked eye. And while it was selfish, it was ignorant too, because she could see things that he did not: there was life beyond rodeo. Even for Bill there would have to be, eventually. And marriage was a compromise—not of himself, but between himself and the something better than he could be on his own. But that was not the way he saw it. When Toni told him she had her own job and her own life, that she was tired of taking care of his affairs, and that she didn't want to go on being married to someone who was never home, she didn't mean she wanted to leave him. She knew that she was young enough to make a new life for herself if she chose to, though by this she imagined a different life with Bill, not one without him. She didn't want a divorce; she didn't believe in divorce. But Bill didn't try to understand.

"At that time she was really just trying to get me to wake up and hear her," he said. "I never knew that for a long time that's all she was doing. She wasn't wanting to have a divorce or anything; she just wanted me to hear her side of it. 'Course, you know when you get going like that and sometimes you get caught up in your own . . ." He paused, shaking his head. There was a sense of remorse as he retold the story—not necessarily that things hadn't worked out with Toni, because everyone found what they needed in the end, but that he had hurt her.

"It was all my fault," he said. "That was just me being a dumb man. If I would have just listened to her, heard her . . . She said, well, she didn't know if she could do it anymore, and I said, 'Okay, that's your choice.' I said, 'You better make up your mind by the time I walk out the door,' and that was too bad because she didn't know. She was confused and reaching out for somebody to understand her, and by the time I figured that out it was too late. So I left and went down and signed the divorce papers and got in my car and left. I love her dearly, but it just didn't work out. She had her own life to live."

He left her the house and everything in it, saying all he needed was his saddle and the car. Their argument sparked enough anger to fuel him out of town, and he felt the self-saving rush of independence as he sped away; it would carry him far enough that by the time he looked back his life with Toni would be out of sight. "I was determined that I didn't need anybody," he said, "that I could do it on my own." Later, he might remember her in lonely moments and miss her in an abstract way. But it was the thought of her he would miss more than anything—the thought of her waiting at home for him, the thought of her hitching her life to his. The thought of her was all he had had from the beginning, a kind of two-dimensional woman who could fit into his life when and where he wanted her and not be a bother in between. Like he said, Toni had her own life to live. And he had his.

Chapter 8

Carole

"I've always been a one-woman man," Bill said. "Nobody believes that, but it's true. I could barely handle one, let alone two. When I was married, I was married; and when I was unmarried, I took up after Carole." He says this in a straightforward manner, as if it is obvious, or should be. In fact, there had been very little of his life that Bill hadn't had a woman—his mother, his older sisters, or his wife—taking care of him, and it is an interesting side to a man who is, in all ways, so independent. For the most part, though, the stories with any racy trim are rare and tame, the kinds of stories any young man has—of getting caught in an elevator with three women in Las Vegas, of his photograph hanging on the wall of a certain cathouse in Montana. Considering his status as a bronc rider and a champion, Bill was a gentleman in comparison with some of his counterparts.

When he met Carole O'Rourke over a cup of coffee in the trailer of their mutual friends Butch and J.C. Bonine, Bill was still married to Toni. But everyone on the circuit, including Carole, knew about his pending divorce. Word traveled fast. Bill's crumbling marriage had disrupted his season, and as of early summer he was trailing the top five bronc riders. Carole O'Rourke was favored to win the 1973 barrel racing world championship. She was almost all leg, very lean, and she wore her wavy, dark hair tied at the nape of her neck—details Bill didn't miss entirely.

Butch and J.C.'s camper was cramped in its efficient way, the walls narrow and everything stacked or folded up against something else. Bill sat in the booth that the table and its padded benches made, pressed against the side wall with his shoulders hunched, cradling his coffee cup between his hands. The trailer was parked in camper village, the lot behind the rodeo arena where the barrel racers and the ropers parked their rigs. Carole and Butch Bonine kept their barrel horses in an adjacent pasture. Ordinarily, it was beneath a bronc rider to be seen with a barrel racer in camper village, but Bill was friends with J.C. Bonine, a saddle bronc rider, whose wife, Butch, was a barrel racer. Although it was the first time that Bill and Carole officially met, he knew who she was, and she certainly knew him. But Bill was hardly sociable. He barely spoke a word to her, even though she was sitting next to him for over an hour, and after Butch had refilled their coffee cups several times over and the day's events had been rehashed, Bill stepped out of the camper through the little latched door with a curt goodnight.

He didn't see Carole again until the beginning of August. On the first night of the competition in Burwell, Nebraska, he recognized her at the entrance to the arena, minutes before the grand entry. The rodeo producer was asking him to take an introduction after the girls galloped around carrying the U.S. and Nebraska state flags. "You can just take one of their horses," the producer said, waving toward the group holding matching palominos. Bill walked casually up to Carole and said, "I'm just going to borrow this girl's horse because she's got long legs and I won't have to change the stirrups." It had only been a month since Butch and J.C. had introduced them, and Carole didn't know what to think of his approaching her. She wasn't sure he remembered her, but he looked like he did. Maybe he was just being practical, like he said. Nonetheless, she felt fluttery, even though she wasn't a fluttery kind of girl, and her response to him was part awkward, part tough. She carried her flag in the grand entry, handed her horse off to Bill, and stood back to watch him gallop effortlessly around the arena while the announcer introduced him: two-time world champion saddle bronc rider from Cody, Wyoming—Cody Bill Smith. The crowd cheered.

Bill had never paid much attention to barrel racing, but that night in Burwell he made an excuse to disappear for a few minutes and find a spot near the rails. He glanced at the alleyway at the north end of the arena every time a girl rode up and stopped a few paces before the starting line to gather her horse. They appeared one at a time, spurred their horses into the arena at an immediate gallop, crossed the starting line, and ran the cloverleaf course—around the barrel on the east side, across the width of the arena and around the west barrel, up to the south end around the third barrel, and back along the length of the arena, crossing over the starting line at the north. If they were good it would take around fifteen seconds, but anywhere from fifteen to twenty seconds was normal; anything less than fifteen seconds was quite good and could usually win money. To make good time, horse and rider had to be fast, precise, and in control. If a barrel was knocked over, five seconds were added to the racer's time as a penalty.

When Carole appeared she was wearing a tall-crowned hat, a pretty western shirt, and buckskin chaps that drew attention to her slim hips; in her teeth she clenched the crop she would need for the home stretch. Printer—her tall, strong, bay gelding with a white star on his forehead—danced back and forth, turning his body sideways to the open gate, straining to run. With one hand Carole held the saddle horn, and with the other she drew the reins in tight to her belly, holding him back from sprinting out into the arena. Bill thought they looked like a good pair.

Carole waited until Printer was solid beneath her, until they were in perfect balance to lunge with full force across the starting line, and then she released the reins slightly. The instant Printer felt her release his mouth he took off toward the first barrel. Carole steered him in a tight path, pulling the reins across his neck to turn him around the barrel as close as they could come without touching it. He dropped his inside shoulder down so far as he turned that his entire body canted at a 45-degree angle; he had the same angle as a baseball player sliding into a base—all the weight on one leg, or in this case two—as if he could slide flat into the sand. Carole tried to stay upright, pushing some of her weight to the outside so they wouldn't fall, and just as it looked like they might, Printer came around through the turn, took his weight on his inside feet, and lifted himself upright. Sitting almost on his haunches for a moment, he lunged forward, clawing at the sand with his forefeet, and rushed across the width of the arena toward the next barrel with an almost desperate urgency. His hooves kicked up clods of dirt that spattered against the arena rails and pinged into the steel barrel. Carole breathed heavily through her mouth, clenching the crop between her teeth, and Printer's nostrils flared with each exhalation. The muscles of his chest and haunches rippled as he moved, taking the weight onto his forelegs and pushing off with his hind legs, like a sprinter crouching down into the blocks and blasting off around the inside corner of a track again and again and again.

Around the third barrel, Carole leaned forward, lifting herself up and out of the saddle like a jockey, gave Printer the full length of the rein, and took the crop from between her teeth, slapping the end against his shoulder. In the space of two seconds they flew down the arena and across the finish line into the alleyway and stopped just before hitting the end wall. Bill exhaled. He had been holding his breath.

U

Carole O'Rourke was born Carole Kuhnert on July 1, 1944, in Mississippi. Her father, Charles Kuhnert, was stationed there with the air force. Less than a year later, Phyllis Lucille Gilbert Kuhnert divorced her husband and took her daughter home to Clyde Park, Montana, where the Gilberts had been homesteading since the turn of the century. Phyllis's parents, Philip Horton Gilbert and Hedwig Lucy Uhl Gilbert, helped take care of Carole.

Phil Gilbert was a stern man. He was all long bones and angular lines accentuated by severe, ramrod-straight posture. He had stony eyes and expressionless lips, a broad forehead, and receding hair. He was strict and worked hard and didn't believe in any nonsense. While Phyllis and her siblings were growing up, Phil loaded them with responsibilities and chores: they ironed and sewed, cooked and cleaned, drove the teams of horses that pulled the machinery that stacked the hay, milked the cows, fed the chickens and the pigs, pumped water from the well, and kept the woodsheds filled. If a telephone call came

Carol O'Rourke and her mother on Dixie, at Philip and Hedwig Gilbert's place
in Clyde Park, Montana, 1945. Collection of Carole Smith.

in for one of the neighbors, Phyllis or her sister Gladys would run the
messages to the neighboring ranch. By the time she was eight years
old, Phyllis knew how to drive the family's Model A Ford.

   Phil Gilbert sent all three of his girls to college, which was quite unusual at the time, though Phyllis quit after two years to marry Charles.
Carole's grandmother, Hedwig, had also attended college, completing

a domestic science course at Montana State in 1910–11. She had a reputation for being an excellent cook and homemaker, and while Carole was in high school Hedwig cooked her lunch every day. "I don't think she ever drove," Carole remembered; "she just [stayed home and] did what Grandpa told her to do." Hedwig was Phil's soft counterpart. She had dark, beautiful, round eyes and thick, luxurious hair, and her skin was flawless even when she grew old.

Carole loved being at her grandparents' house. She took volumes of Longfellow from the shelf and memorized his poems, and she played with her grandmother's knick-knacks, especially the miniature horses Hedwig collected. Carole wasn't sure if her grandmother loved horses as much as she did, but when Carole was in high school Hedwig did something extraordinary. What Carole wanted more than anything in the world was her own horse, but neither she nor her mother, Phyllis, nor Phyllis's new husband, John O'Rourke, could afford one. So Hedwig secretly gave her granddaughter $350. "Don't tell your grandfather," Hedwig said to Carole; "he wouldn't approve." As Carole tells it, Phil Gilbert would have thought $350 "a lot of money to spend on foolishness," but he never found out about it.

With the money, Carole bought a three-and-a-half-year-old half-thoroughbred mare called Doubt Me. She was a young horse, fast and difficult to handle, and she had never been used for barrel racing before. At first Carole would run the mare into an arena, and, ignoring the barrels, the horse would take a lap around the fence line at a full gallop while Carole held the reins in one hand and the saddle horn in the other, pulling furiously on the bit and trying desperately to not fall off. But slowly, with her stepfather's help, Carole trained the aptly named Doubt Me to run the pattern of the barrel race without knocking the three barrels over. Once she had accomplished that, she ran the mare faster and faster until she could take the course in decent time. Carole started taking Doubt Me to rodeo competitions and won a good deal. It was the only real happiness of her day to come home from school and race her horse. And it was an accomplishment; prior to her experience with Doubt Me, besides riding as a girl and participating in 4-H, Carole had no background in training barrel horses at all.

When she finished high school, Carole went to Montana State University in Bozeman on a small rodeo scholarship and took Doubt Me with her. Soon after, Doubt Me developed azaturia and could not race anymore. Carole found a stud horse to breed with Doubt Me and named the colt Printer. Printer looked like he would be a good horse, but he wouldn't be ready to ride for another three or four years. In the meantime, Carole leased a horse called Buck, a homely buckskin mare. Everyone who saw them would laugh—at Buck for being so ugly and at Carole for riding such a bad-looking horse. But Buck was fast, and Carole won so much that she went to the College National Finals Rodeo and won the national intercollegiate all-around cowgirl title in 1966.

"That was when I really came out of my shell," Carole remembered. "I actually did better in college than I did in high school in terms of grades; I was really shy in high school, didn't have a lot of confidence. But then when I started barrel racing I met a lot of people who had the same interests as me. I found my niche, I guess." Carole studied elementary education, and when she graduated, she and a girlfriend got teaching jobs in Prescott, Arizona. They wanted a change of scenery, and they figured it would be nice to go somewhere warm. Carole taught third grade for two years in Prescott, then came back to Montana for a year. The following year, she and three of her girlfriends applied for jobs in Yuma, Arizona. By that time, Printer was four years old and ready to ride. Carole took him with her and trained him to run barrels, and at the end of two years she came home again.

Her dream, she had always thought, was to live on a ranch and ride her horses, preferably as far from other people as possible. She had never entirely grown out of her shyness, and, more than the glitter of any town, she liked best the open sky and endless plain. Soon after she returned to Montana, she fell in love with a rancher from back east who had bought a nice spread of land—a big, isolated ranch near Billings. It seemed, at first, like the ideal life; she spent most of the week on the ranch with the rancher, teaching in Billings on the weekdays, and in her spare time she took Printer to rodeos. But Carole wasn't sure the rancher was happy about her rodeoing on the weekends, or perhaps he wasn't satisfied having to compete for her attention. "I think it intimidated him a little bit," she said. Nonetheless, he had asked her to marry him. It was the first real relationship she'd had.

"We had the engagement all announced; that's how close we were," she said, "and then this girl from the past showed up—you know, one of those deals. I heard she was coming back, and I loaded up my horse. Thank goodness I had my horse, and I had my mom." It was August when Carole called her mother and said, "Mom, we're going to rodeo." Days later, they drove to Colorado in Carole's camper with the horse trailer attached to the back. On the weekends Carole entered whatever fair rodeo she could find; Phyllis helped her drive, slept beside her in the tiny confines of the camper, and helped her feed and groom Printer and prepare for each rodeo. They were familiar with each other in this way, in this routine. Phyllis had driven Carole to rodeos in high school and accompanied her in college, and she was still happy to travel with her twenty-eight-year-old daughter in the summer of 1972 after the disappointment of her broken engagement.

John O'Rourke, Carole's stepfather, was supportive too. He had treated Carole like a daughter from the time he married Phyllis, and he was selflessly encouraging of her rodeo career. "He did everything he could to make sure I got to as many rodeos as I could," Carole said. "And it was hard for him." Phyllis and John had three children after they married, and John worked constantly to provide for them all. He worked as a carpenter during the day and came home and milked cows at night and in the mornings, and after a long week's work he'd take Carole to rodeos on the weekends. It was perfectly reasonable to John that his wife should be away for a month with Carole in 1972, and he took care of the house and chores without complaint. But after a month, Phyllis had had enough; it was time, she said, for her to return to her house and her husband, and Carole turned the outfit north without any questions and took her back to Montana. That fall, Carole worked in Billings as a substitute teacher, so she could spend more time on the road. Printer was proving himself to be strong, fast, and smart. They were winning almost everywhere they went, and Carole started to think that, if she dedicated herself to it full-time, she and

Printer could make it to the National Finals Rodeo. As winter came, she decided she would try.

U

Carole hadn't seen Bill since the Burwell rodeo when she ran into him in Omaha, but then they hardly had time to talk. Bill was entered in two rodeos that weekend—in Omaha and Memphis—and he had chartered a plane to fly him between the two. It was nearly the end of the season, and he was in tight competition with his friend John McBeth and the Australian Darrell Kong for the lead going into the Finals. His goal in the last weeks of competition was to gain a comfortable lead. He got on his first horse in Omaha and scored 58 points, then flew to Memphis and won third place for the day, flew back to Omaha and won the next two days and was second in the average, returned to Memphis to win the last day and the average there, and then continued on to Oklahoma City, where he won both days and the average. By week's end Bill had gained a lead of $3,500. With the money, he bought a big new Buick sedan. It was a carbon copy of his old car in a nice dirt-brown color, but this new one didn't have 250,000 miles clocked on the odometer. Bill liked the comfort of the big Buicks; he thought they were the most comfortable car on the market for someone who had to drive as fast and as far as he did all the time.

In late October Carole was carrying a bale of hay through camper village at the Cow Palace in San Francisco. Bill had no reason to be in camper village, but he stopped and leaned out the open window of his new Buick. Strands of hay clung to Carole's shirt and jeans, and her hair fell in her face. Bill said, "Oh, just throw it on up there on the trunk and I'll carry it over for you." She was hesitant to put a bale of hay on the trunk of his obviously new car, certain it would scratch the paint. But he insisted. He took her to her trailer, and she introduced him to Printer. They talked for awhile that day and saw each other almost every day after for the rest of the week. By week's end, they were each the leading money-winners in their respective events and were both favored to win world championship titles.

Carole O'Rourke on Printer at the National Finals Rodeo, 1973. Photo by Bern Gregory. Courtesy of the National Cowboy and Western Heritage Museum, Oklahoma City.

A month later in Oklahoma City at the National Finals, practically guaranteed to win the championship, Bill was feeling sick. He had a sore throat and a slight fever. Carole was concerned about Printer, whose legs were sore. She had noticed that he was losing speed coming out of his turns. The Finals lasted nine days, and by the middle of the week Carole was falling behind and Bill was holding his lead by only a thread. On the seventh day, Bill turned his horse out. He was too sick to ride, a situation he almost never found himself in. When a cowboy turned a horse out and didn't ride, he got no points for the day, took an automatic last place, and earned no money. On the eighth day he turned out again and stayed in his motel room too tired to eat, too feverish to sleep. With one night of competition to go, he had to make a choice: either he had to ride to win or he had to concede the title. If he didn't ride the ninth round, he was sure to lose the gold buckle. He chose to ride. The bronc called X-9 was his draw, and Bill rode for a score of 86 points, a score only two other rides earned at the Finals that year. After one last ride—a tenth-round, 76-point ride on Copenhagen Cyclone—Bill closed his season with yearly winnings of $26,069, earning the world championship buckle. X-9 was a notoriously tough horse, and Bill's ride was a signature of his career. It was a beautiful ride, powerful and picture perfect, and it was accomplished under great physical strain and emotional pressure.

That night of his third championship, Bill invited everyone to his hotel room for a room party, and everyone came to celebrate his win. In the midst of the festivities, in front of the assembled mass, Bill's best friends quieted the crowd to present him with a special award. They were honored, they said, to be with Bill on such an important evening and were proud of his accomplishments, among them his third world championship saddle bronc title. But in addition to this honor, they wanted to add another: the Hoof Pick Award. Someone held a small plaque aloft, a professional-looking plaque to which Bill's friends had attached a hoof pick and a small brass plate on which they had engraved "Hoof Pick Award, 1973, Bill Smith." There was no such official thing as the Hoof Pick Award, but everyone got the joke immediately. Bill Smith, the bronc rider, had been caught carrying a bale of hay on the trunk of his new car, which could only mean he had taken up with a barrel racer. And every bronc rider knew that as soon as a cowboy took up with a barrel racer he would soon be taking care of that girl's horse. Taking care of a horse meant having daily chores and a schedule; it meant traveling slower; it meant having a real responsibility, sometimes as mundane as cleaning the dirt from a horse's hooves. Bill, however embarrassed, accepted the plaque graciously and in good humor.

In the morning, Carole went back to Livingston with Phyllis and John. She had come in third at the Finals, and while she was disappointed at not having won, she was more worried about her horse than anything else. She left Printer and her camper with a friend in Oklahoma, so she wouldn't have to haul the horses in the cold over snowy mountain passes. Bill, still feeling sick, decided he would stay in Oklahoma City until Monday. He thought he had the flu and that a day of rest in bed would do him good. But Monday night came, and he felt worse. Everyone had left town. "I got scared," he said, "and there wasn't anybody there. So I said, well, I will go get in my car and drive to Dallas. Shawn Davis lived in Dallas, right north of Dallas. I thought I'd go to Shawn's place, the closest person I knew. You're in Oklahoma City, you think it's just a little hop and a skip to Dallas, but it's 190 miles." By the time he got there he felt awful. And Shawn wasn't home. "So I had this lady friend in Dallas, a school teacher, and she was the only [other] person I knew. I called her up, and I told her I wanted to come over. Of course I didn't tell her I was sick." Sarah, the lady friend, told Bill to come over, and when he got there she could see immediately that he was in bad shape. She put him to bed and left him there the next day when she went to school. Bill deteriorated over the course of the day, and, assuming he would feel better eventually if he just got some rest, he stayed in bed and waited. "I remember having to go to the bathroom," he said, "and behind the commode was a closet. I remember going into the bathroom, looking in the mirror, and the next thing I know I'm laying on my back in her closet looking up at all them dresses. I had no idea where I was or what had happened, and I was laying there when she came walking in and found me."

The sight of him splayed out in her bathroom understandably unnerving, Sarah put Bill in her car and took him straight to the emergency room. By the time they got there, his throat was abnormally swollen and his jaw was locked shut. An intern took Bill's vitals and said he thought it was tonsillitis, but he wasn't sure. The intern said he could give Bill a shot of antibiotics and by morning he would be fine, but it was possible that it wasn't tonsillitis, in which case he didn't want to give Bill the shot. This hemming and hawing was not the answer Bill was looking for. He wanted a quick fix. He told Sarah he wanted to go somewhere else, to find a doctor who would give him a shot and make him feel better immediately. It was four o'clock in the morning when they got back in the car and drove to the emergency room at Baylor. When they were finally attended to, Sarah told the doctor she thought Bill had tonsillitis and they gave him a shot. "Well," he said, "by the next morning I was fine, and that night I was in the emergency room. Surgery. They had to send to Chicago for an antibiotic. I had a bug in there that they hadn't seen since World War II. They drained a pint of serum off that abscess in my throat, and the serum, they said, one drop of it in my bloodstream and I was dead." The Cow Palace, which was used as a staging ground for troops and supplies during World War II, was also home to livestock much of the year. Unlikely as it seemed, perhaps he had picked up the unusual bug there.

Bill stayed in the hospital until after Christmas. Sarah called his family in Cody to tell them where he was, and Bill's brother Jim flew to Dallas to stay with him in the hospital and to drive the Buick home. On New Year's Eve, Bill was released from the hospital, and the next day he flew back to Wyoming. He went home to the house he had bought for Toni, but Toni was still living there, and it wasn't really his home anymore. He had lost over ten pounds and was weak and tired and uncomfortable. "I had this apparatus I had to irrigate my throat. I had to stick a hose down my throat once or twice a day and pour white vinegar down there and flush out the abscess," he said. "It was a stinkin' hard deal to do. And so when I got to Toni's, and our deal was not good, I was very uncomfortable and she was uncomfortable." He knew he had to leave, but he didn't know where to go. "I was sick, and our marriage was gone. Toni was trying to make a new life for herself. I didn't want to be there. So I called Carole."

U

"After I came home I never did hear anything from Bill, and I thought that was kind of strange," Carole said. "I'd gone out with him quite a bit at the Finals, but I figured, well . . ." She paused and shrugged, as if to say it would have been understandable, she would have understood, if they'd had a fling and then he'd gotten back on the road. But it would have been strange, considering the way they had been together. It didn't seem to add up. Of course, she didn't know he was sick. When he called and explained what happened, it made sense. And it made sense that she should pick him up in Cody, that he would leave his ex-wife's house and come to live with her, that he would understand when she said they had to drive first to Oklahoma to get her horses and then to Arizona so she could teach. "I had my camper and a horse trailer and my pickup, so I always had my home with me," she said. Bill settled in to the cramped living quarters, the bed above the dining table next to the kitchen with all its latched cabinets just feet away from the door.

Carole took care of him that whole spring, took him back to Dallas so he could get his tonsils taken out, and nursed him through his recuperation. "I couldn't swallow because of the tonsils," he said, "and Carole learned how to make egg custard. I still love her egg custard." From then on they were together. "I guess we had some things in common," Carole said. "It sure wasn't my looks, that's for sure." She is a pretty woman but not flashy like a buckle bunny. Nor did she have the air of worldly sophistication that airline stewardesses picked up in their travels. She was simple in her desires—to have a piece of land somewhere pretty, to have horses. "Maybe he wanted a horsey girl, I don't know. Seemed like whenever we were together we were always talking about horses." They were also similarly quiet, loyal, stubborn, and determined. When Bill was presented the gold buckle he had won at the National Finals at the Denver Stock Show in January 1974, he gave it to Carole, and she "thought that was something." She continued to take care of him even after he was able to ride again and took off down the road in late spring.

Carole continued to barrel race with Printer, although his legs were bothering him more and more. Eventually, she took him to a veterinarian in Houston, and he was diagnosed with navicular, a common and now easily treated problem of which not much was understood at the time. "At that time navicular was the kiss of death," Carole said. She gave him painkillers and raced with him through the spring, but the condition only worsened. After the Fourth of July she retired him, and, unable to find another horse like him, she acknowledged the end of her professional barrel racing career. She took a job teaching in Cody that fall, where she and Bill decided they would establish a home base. It was only four hours from her mom, and there was plenty of work to be found there.

Chapter 9

Bulletproof

When Bill rode his first bronc of 1974 on March 1 in Scottsdale, Arizona, there was no predicting what his next two years had in store. The two months of bed rest since the 1973 National Finals might have cost him more than he knew, since he was used to moving constantly on horseback or afoot. When he wasn't on a bronc he was usually playing football with the boys, in any field or pasture they could find, and the running kept him in good shape for the rodeo. Two months laid up might have weakened him. His back had started to hurt when he drove and when he slept. The constant pain started to give him headaches. He dropped from first in the world to sixth, and the following year he dropped another place, to seventh. By the spring of 1976, he was being carried out of the arena nearly every ride.

That spring, Bill, his brother Rick, and J.C. Bonine left Cody together for Redding, California. They were driving the little brown half-ton pick-up that the Dodge Corporation had given Bill to drive as an endorsement, but riding in it was starting to be a real problem. The long hours in the cab made him uncomfortable, and sometimes his legs would go numb for a few seconds at a time. He had to stop every so often to get out and stretch. Despite this, they kept going down the road. They got on their broncs in Redding, and Bill won, and they turned right around for Chickasha, Oklahoma, nearly eighteen hundred miles from Redding, more than twenty-four hours away.

In Chickasha, Bill drew a little, mediocre mare. Rick and J.C. helped him set his saddle and lower himself into the chute. He took

Bill Smith on Old Shep at the National Finals Rodeo, 1975, with Shawn Davis (*far right*) judging, and (*from left*) Joe Alexander (five-time bareback world champion), Bobby Berger (1980 world champion), Rusty Riddle, and Ace Berry. Photo by Jerry and Emmy Gustafson. Collection of Bill Smith.

his rein and felt the mare uneasy beneath him, and he waited to nod his head for the gate. As he waited for her to settle, he talked to her softly and stroked her just above the withers, and just as he thought she was beginning to settle, she lunged ahead in the chute, giving them no room to recover. In that instant, as the little horse lunged, the gate flew open and she took a leap out into the arena. The force of her leap tossed Bill across her back like a rag. His legs went numb. His hand on the braided rein was the only grip he had on the little mare until, a moment later, he let go and hit the ground. Rick and J.C. jumped the arena fence and helped him out, his arms across their shoulders. They took him back to the motel and laid him on the bed. The pain came in spasms, and the numbness came in spurts, and in the moments of normalcy he could get around in stiff, careful movements. The next day, they drove two hundred miles to Fort Smith, Arkansas.

Bill drew a nice horse in Fort Smith. He settled into his saddle and took up his rein, and the horse jumped, just hopped in the chute before they opened the gate. This time Bill's left side went numb, his hand and his left leg, "just like a lick, like somebody had shot electricity through them," he said. His rein dropped to the ground, and he followed it. The little horse kicked off to the far wall.

Laying in the dust was not the perspective from which Bill liked to see the world, and it was clear to him at that moment that something had to be done. The pain was impeding his winning, and that was unacceptable. He went home and did some investigating. He got advice, solicited and not, from everybody. They all told him, no matter what, not to let anyone operate on his back. So he tried a chiropractor, but that didn't work. And then he tried acupuncture; a new doctor in Cody was doing it, so he gave it a whirl. He went through ten or fifteen treatments during the month of June; "I mean I looked like a pine tree he stuck so many needles in me," he said. He didn't drive, and he didn't ride; he just lay still and rested for the entire month. By the end of June he felt as good as new, just in time for the rash of rodeos around the Fourth of July, so he optimistically entered Cody, Laramie, Sheridan, and Calgary.

At the Cody Fourth of July Rodeo, Bill drew the same good horse that had dumped him at Fort Smith. He got on and rode the horse easily, and he thought to himself, "Man, I'm healed!" But he was stiff again when he got to Laramie, 400 miles southeast. The horse he had there scattered out across the big arena. When the whistle blew, Bill's legs were shot, and he'd already launched out of the saddle into the dirt. They drove to Sheridan, 330 miles to the north, and Bill drew a nice horse he'd ridden a dozen times. He got on her, and with one jump she threw him sky high. Still determined, he got in the truck and drove to Calgary—670 miles.

Prominent lawyers and doctors composed the rodeo committee in Calgary, all nice gentlemen Bill had come to know over the years through his friend the Canadian bronc rider Winston Bruce. The committee thought fondly of their native son Winston, and any friend of Winston's was a friend of the committee. When Bill lit out in the

Calgary arena, his first horse throwing him in a sloppy wreck, one of the doctors came running. He looked at Bill and said, "I've seen enough of this." The doctor knew what happened to bronc riders who rode through serious injuries, and instead of letting Bill ride his next go-round, he drove Bill directly to the Foothills Hospital and left him in the care of nurses with an appointment for a mylogram. The doctor had a perspective on the situation that Bill could not have: he knew Bill would continue to ride because he thought he could and because he thought he had to, because there was no money to pay the medical bills and because he thought he was indestructible. After Russ's oil rig accident, the avalanche, his own illness, he might have seen warnings: accidents happen even to the best of men; the body is not unbreakable; illness and recovery can be costly. Instead, the incidents served as proof, not warnings. Bill was thirty-five years old, and he never thought he would live past thirty. He had been lucky all his life, luckier than he thought possible. He had already lived five years longer than he thought he would, which made every extra minute feel like borrowed time. One day his luck would run out and it would be over, and he told his friends he hoped they wouldn't be with him when it happened. But all these surface thoughts, ideas in the abstract, didn't deepen with the serious situation at hand. In Calgary, Bill was thinking about a paycheck.

Alone in the hospital with his boots by his bedside, Bill's spinal fluid was drawn, a dye was injected in its place, and X-rays were taken of his neck and spine. He was ordered to keep still, flat on his back, for forty-eight hours, while the hole in his spine healed. Eight hours later Bill got his draw: his next horse at Calgary was a good one. He begged and pleaded and sweet-talked and crooned, but the nurses wouldn't release him. They shook their heads and closed the door to his little room.

Bill didn't consider any consequences. He found his clothes and got dressed, called Carol Bruce, Winston's wife, and told her where to fetch him. She came, as he asked, and drove him, perhaps against her better judgment, back to the arena. Standing or sitting in any position with his head elevated, Bill could last about ten minutes. The ensuing headache at the end of that time was worse than any of the pain he'd withstood so far. When the headache began, he would squat down with his head between his knees, butt in the air, for two or three minutes. When the pain subsided, he'd go a little further. Finally behind the chutes, he had his friends put his saddle on his bronc. They secured his rigging and had him all ready to go while he put his chaps on and then lay down, put one boot on and lay down, put the other boot on and lay down. When they called his name, he jumped up and climbed over the chute. All in one motion he took his stirrups and rein, nodded his head, and went out the gate on thirteen hundred pounds of flesh.

The horse lunged, and Bill followed, thrusting his heels into the muscled shoulders, raising his right hand high in the air. The horse's front hooves slammed into the dirt and sank, the chest and shoulders taking the impact and the weight of the beast and Bill on its back. Bill's spurs caught and held him in the saddle as the horse bucked, throwing its hind feet out behind and up into the air in a forceful punch. Bill's free arm flew back. The horse came down on his haunches and pushed off. Bill's heels swept toward the saddle. His hand moved in and back with the motion of the horse's head; his free arm waved forward, as deliberate and graceful as a tightrope walker on a rope shaken violently in every direction. Again the front hooves slammed into the sand. Again Bill's heels and hands whipped into position, followed the motion, corrected for imbalance. Six seconds, and it was a beautiful ride. His head was pounding, pounding with every muscle's movement, every beat of blood and breath, his and the horse's, both bodies fighting with and against the other. Eight seconds, and he hardly heard the whistle; the pain in his head was so audible, screaming. But he was still there. The pick-up men plucked him off the horse and deposited him safely on the ground. The horse went off kicking and was herded out of the arena. The judges delivered their numbers, and the scores were raised in the air, the score for the fierceness of the horse and the score for the grace of its rider, and the numbers were added together. Bill won the go-round for a prize of $600, and all he wanted was to go home.

A friend who had a van with a bed in it agreed to haul Bill as far as Billings. All the way, Bill lay with his head hung over the edge of the bed taking the painkillers they'd given him at the hospital to no effect. Carole rescued him in Billings and took him home again. "The mylogram trick—Carole knew just what I'd done," he said. "I didn't have to tell her." And yet he knew that he couldn't ignore the injury any longer; something serious had to be done.

In the old days, pre-1976, a cowboy couldn't afford to be crippled. Up until that point the PRCA had offered its members no insurance plan in case of accident or injury. But just before Bill's accident, the PRCA raised its membership fees and, at the cowboys' request, instituted an insurance policy. Bill's policy covered $250 a week for the duration of his disability, so long as he was injured in the arena and could prove it. And so long as the arena was in the United States. This last stipulation was a sticking point. So far, his only serious injury requiring hospitalization had occurred in Canada. But not anticipating the injury in Calgary, Bill had already signed up for the rodeo in Cheyenne. All he needed to do was get on one more bronc. He would fall before the whistle, they would take him to the hospital, and, seeing that he was injured, he would be eligible for insurance.

U

Before he left for Cheyenne, Bill called his friend Paul Mayo in Texas and explained the situation. Bill said he was going to need surgery; there was no doubt about it. His legs were going numb for periods of ten to fifteen minutes, and the rest of the time it just hurt more than he could bear. He told Paul he was starting to get scared, that it was looking more and more like he would need an operation. Bill said that if he had to have anyone operate on his back, there was only one man in America he would trust to do it.

In the late 1960s, when Bill's career was taking off, he had met Walt Garrison through their mutual friend C. R. Boucher in Wichita Falls, Texas. Walt had just been drafted by the Dallas Cowboys out of Oklahoma State. He supplemented his football salary by steer wrestling, a skill he learned as a boy on his Uncle Leroy's farm near Lewisville,

Texas. Walt only had time for thirty or thirty-five rodeos a year, at least half of what was necessary for top-tier distinction, but he was one of the most determined and physically strong people Bill knew. Walt was likewise admiring of Bill's toughness and his rising status, and the two men quickly became friends. At Walt's side Bill met the Cowboys, and, by virtue of the personal connection, he became a fervent fan. He followed the statistics as closely as he followed his horses, and his traveling companions came to understand that to go down the road with him meant stopping anywhere under any circumstances to watch a game, even if it meant bedding down forty miles outside of their destination. Bill told Paul Mayo that he wanted an appointment with the Dallas Cowboys' orthopedic physician, Dr. J. Pat Evans. He was the only man Bill knew who would understand the physical strain he put on his body every day and the fact that he wanted to carry on as he had been for many more years. He didn't want a quick fix, nor did he want anyone telling him to slow down. Paul Mayo, who still saw Walt Garrison often, said he'd see what he could do.

The next day, Bill left for Cheyenne with his nephews Tom and Bruce Keller. Bill had drawn a prototype bucking horse—just the kind of horse he loved—a big, strong gelding who stood stock still in the chute and bucked fair and square. Bill's saddle fit the horse perfectly. Tom and Bruce helped him into the chute, and as he was reaching to put his foot in the stirrup he hesitated. He looked down at the strength of the horse and saw the wreck that was coming, and then just as suddenly his instincts told him otherwise. As he settled into the saddle, the horse felt perfect. The elation of a beautiful ride overwhelmed him and overrode all the present and projected pain. As he nodded his head, he couldn't help himself; he had to ride this horse. He would win this one and get thrown off the next. He would ride this horse, just this one, and he would win.

The gate swung open, and the horse reared out in a fabulous arc. The energy was electric, a pure surge of adrenaline. Bill's back went out and his legs went numb and his entire body followed a trajectory influenced by but independent of the horse's motion, uncontrolled and uncontrollable, until it collided with the dry, dank earth. He didn't have to fall. Tom and Bruce dragged him out of the arena and took him home. He'd warned them that he didn't want an ambulance and he didn't want to go to the hospital. He didn't want anyone to touch him except Dr. Evans. If there was one person who was going to understand the physical wear and tear of his body, his mindset and mechanics, he thought it would be Evans. Paul Mayo had made the necessary arrangements. Bill got his referral, picked up the X-rays from his mylogram, and got on an airplane.

Three days later in Dallas, in the heat of August, Dr. Evans looked over the X-rays from Calgary. Typically, a doctor asks a set of questions to determine the best course of action for the surgeon to take on behalf of his patient. Does the patient expect a complete cure? What percentage of improvement could he live with? What percentage of improvement would he be happy with? What things does the patient have trouble with now or cannot do that he would want most to be able to do? Can he accept the possibility of extended physical therapy or rehabilitation? When is he likely to have to return to work? Evans had a good idea of what he was dealing with. He looked at Bill laid up in bed and simply said, "Now, what are you planning to do?" Bill didn't think twice. He replied, "I want to ride broncs in Denver, Colorado, in January." Evans nodded and slipped the X-rays back in their envelope. He said, "Okay, that's what I wanted to hear," and scheduled Bill for surgery the next day.

That night Bill was wheeled into a room with five other men. They were all scheduled for back surgery the next day, and Evans came to see them just before he went home for the night. He wanted to remind them that there was only a 30 percent success ratio with the surgery they were about to undertake and a 50 percent chance they might never walk again. He said he wanted them to sleep on these facts, to weigh the costs and benefits, as they saw them, for each of their situations. When Bill woke up the next morning, he was the only one left in the room. If he was scared by the probability of never walking again, he was probably more afraid of the possibility of not being able to ride. In his mind at the time there was no distinction between the two. It was a short-sighted view but also understandable: ask a man to live without the one thing he most enjoys in life, his passion and the thing that also happens to be his livelihood, and he will probably have to think twice. In pain and on a losing streak, the fifty-fifty odds Bill faced going into surgery looked to him like a glass half full. As scheduled, he went in for his operation. They fused three vertebrae of his lower back into one solid line, and it went smoothly, without any complication.

Paul Mayo was out of town at the time, but he had told the girl he was living with that Bill was having surgery, and on the day that Bill was released from the hospital, she was there to meet him. Bill thought she was an angel. She took him home and put him in her bed and stayed with him for a week. The doctor had forbidden Bill from doing anything; he was not to carry even a shaving kit. A week later he was able to fly home and begin six months of rehabilitation. He walked a mile every day and did exactly what Evans told him to do. After two check-ups, Evans was very pleased with the job.

Years later, with a shrug and a smirk, Bill admits the story sounds outrageous. But his body language suggests that it also seems perfectly natural. Bronc riders, like running backs, assume a certain set of conventions when they decide to ride or play: they will put themselves in harm's way; they may get hurt in the process; they are willing to sacrifice their bodies for their sport. And if every time they called for the gate or set foot on the field they thought about the risk they were about to take, they would likely fail. Instead, they thought about the perfect ending—a touchdown, or an eighty-six-point ride. "You get to thinking you're bulletproof," Bill said. "That's a mindset. In order to put yourself at that physical risk and stay on that high, competitive edge all the time, you've got to be that way." Casey Tibbs put it this way: "Twice in my life I thought about getting hurt as I came out of the chute. If I ever feel like that a third time, I'll quit."

"That was very stupid," Bill said, referring not to the mindset but to the chain of decisions he made in the spring and summer of 1977. "I could have ended up in a wheelchair or dead, but at the time I needed $600. It didn't seem like anything out of the ordinary to me then; it's what I'd been doing my whole life—getting on bucking horses and trying to win." By some strokes of luck and some forces of determination, six months after his surgery Bill was headed to the Denver rodeo as he said he would be. On January 10, Bill rode his first bronc of the new year. He had never been so happy to get on a bronc in his life. It wasn't a great ride, but it didn't hurt. Five days later, Walt Garrison helped the Cowboys crush the Broncos 27–10 in Super Bowl XII. Bill was fully recovered and headed into what would be the last and greatest year of his career.

Chapter 10

A Life of Magic

Bill turned thirty-seven years old in 1978. He had been riding broncs for twenty years, eighteen years as a professional rodeo cowboy, and he considered every year of his professional career to be an improvement on the last. He had gone to the National Finals Rodeo thirteen times in fourteen years, missing only one year due to injury. He had won three world championship buckles for saddle bronc riding, a feat few men had accomplished. With each year that went by he had improved his accidental style, and by 1978 he considered himself to be at the top of his game. Winston Bruce said that one of the distinguishing things about Bill's career was that he got better every year he rode. "If I hadn't gotten any better it would have been very sad," Bill said, "because I wasn't very good when I started." By 1978 he had accomplished more than he ever thought he would.

Since his back surgery, Bill had decided to slow down considerably. Instead of their usual ninety to a hundred rodeos, he and his traveling companions—Mel Hyland, the 1972 and 1976 world champion, and J.C. Bonine, the 1977 world champion—went to only sixty or seventy rodeos in 1978, taking more time to rest and spending more time at home. "I was just in control of everything those last two or three years," Bill said. "I just went out, rode, had fun, relaxed." He also made a serious effort to be with Carole in Cody, where she was teaching elementary school, and he spent a good deal of time helping his youngest brother, Rick, with his rodeo career. By year's end, Rick had clinched a gold buckle at the College National Finals Rodeo.

Bill Smith on Mainliner at the National Finals Rodeo, 1978. Photo by Randy and Karen Huffman. Collection of Bill Smith.

Bill, for his part, won more important rodeos in 1978 than he had ever won in a single year.

But it was watching his brother and the other young cowboys coming up that made Bill start to think seriously about retirement. By 1978 most of his competition was ten years his junior, kids in their twenties who were just starting out. They had the fearless, selfish desire to ride and to win, the ability to go without food and sleep and to bounce back from injury. At the 1978 National Finals, a bronc rider not much older than Rick—the twenty-three-year-old Joe Marvel—blew the competition away and won the world. Joe Marvel was only going to get better, and Bill knew he was not going to be able to compete. But despite all of his success in rodeo, there was no saved money on which to retire, or even enough to take a break between rodeo and the next thing. Bill was not yet forty years old; he had never held a steady job, never had a boss, and had no college degree. Besides his saddle, spurs, and car, the only thing of any value he owned was a four-hundred-acre plot of land in Bridger, Montana, that he'd bought for $20,000 in 1968. And yet, he knew retirement was imminent. A man couldn't afford to stay on the circuit and live comfortably if he wasn't winning. Going down the road was physically and financially draining, and at thirty-seven years old, Bill liked to get a decent night's sleep in a real bed instead of driving three hundred miles through the night. He preferred to eat three meals a day, seven days a week. More important, the extreme physicality of the sport put aging muscles, joints, bones, and tendons at great risk, and for a man who would never have a desk job, thirty-seven was awfully young to be physically disabled.

As much as Bill knew his time was coming, he wanted to make sure he went out satisfied so nothing would tempt him to come back. He knew so many cowboys who retired only to reappear for one more shot and guys who hung on too long, embarrassing themselves in a series of bad-to-worse performances. There were also those who, not knowing what to do without the structure of the season, drank themselves sick or lost their money gambling. After twenty years of constant companionship, adventure, freedom, and free will, leaving the circuit was hard. There was no question that retirement was a risk. But at least Bill didn't have the problem of potentially squandering a small fortune; he had no money to start with.

"It's a hard transition," Bill said, "for a person to go from rodeo, or I'm sure any athletics, into the normal. You spend every bit of your concentration, energy, time, thought in trying to learn how to ride and win and be a bronc rider, or whatever it is, and then it's over and you're in your late thirties and you have to start out in the real world, in the mainstream, competing with people fifteen to twenty years younger than you, and you have no background. You're just twenty years late. And you're used to being in the spotlight; you're used to doing anything you want, making your own decisions, no bosses. It's the most free way of life there is. If you're fortunate enough to be able

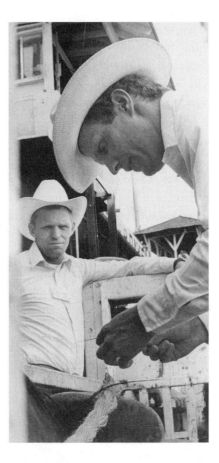

Watching the next generation of cowboys—Bill Smith looks on as Rick Smith sets his rigging, Cheyenne, Wyoming, 1985. Collection of Bill Smith.

to win, you can say what you want, do what you want, and all you have to do is ride good and you're fine; you don't have to be diplomatic, you don't have to be nice unless you want to; you can tell anybody to kiss your behind; and if you ride good, you still can win. It's not that way in real life. You've got to interact with people and treat people good, even sometimes when you don't think you should. But you have to learn that. Rodeo, as great as it is and as wonderful as it is, it's not real life. It's a life of magic for a young man who can win, and I can't imagine any thing being better than that, but it's not the real world.

"One thing I always knew was that I didn't want to hang on past when I should. I had witnessed some of my heroes stay on too long just for the money or whatever, past their prime. I was very, very proud of what I'd done, and I was no way going to stay around and tarnish my accomplishments—they were far, far and away more than I ever dreamed I could do. I was completely happy."

On a personal level, Bill was thinking about asking Carole to marry him. But facing the real world meant acknowledging that he didn't have much to offer by way of security at that moment. He had no money and only the possibility of a job producing a rodeo with some businessmen in North Platte, Nebraska. Carole was still teaching in Cody, living in a tiny trailer from which Bill would come and go. She was happy there and she had her own friends, but she was always waiting for him to come home, and she was sometimes keeping him afloat. They had been together for six years, since the 1973 National Finals, and had rarely discussed the procedural matter of meeting the preacher. But this steady, hard-working woman, Bill knew, would be strong and would stand by his side even in tough times. She already had. She was quite familiar with the realities of their situation, and she would not answer blindly or with any delusions of grandeur. There was no question that she loved him, and that he loved her, that they were each others' ideal companions, and that they would stand by each other through everything. The ceremony of marriage, in Bill's mind, was a procedural operation and would have little actual effect on their lives together, but it was, he knew, the proper thing to do. This is what Bill figured one afternoon while they were having coffee: he had been lucky many times in his life, but Carole was the luckiest thing that had ever happened to him, and it seemed as good a turning point as any, a fine time to stop going down the road, to have a home, and to think about the rest of his life.

"So what does it take to get married?" he said.

"You're the one who's done it before. You ought to know," she answered.

And there it was, settled.

"I guess we talked about it for a little while, but that was about it," Carole said. They called some friends and family together, and between Bill, Carole, and the friends who stood up with them, they barely had enough money to pay the preacher. Carole wore a purple dress that fell at her mid-calf, and the ceremony was short and characteristically utilitarian. They went home together to the trailer outside of Cody, and nothing much changed after the wedding as far as their circumstances were concerned.

U

That winter Bill was invited to compete in an exhibition rodeo. Walt Garrison, who had become the spokesman for Copenhagen-Skoal tobacco, organized a match competition between the top fifteen bronc riders of 1978 and that year's college champion for a purse larger than any offered in history—$18,500. In 1978 Bill's yearly winnings had been just under $30,000; relatively speaking, even a portion of the Copenhagen-Skoal's purse would be a gold mine. He was the oldest invited competitor, and he felt his chances of winning were slim, but it was too big a chance to pass up. He sent in the $500 entry fee and bought a plane ticket to Fort Worth on his credit card. Carole couldn't afford to go with him. But Bill made a deal with himself and told Carole that he would retire after the Copenhagen-Skoal, no matter what happened. He spent the intervening months competing in the usual circuit rodeos, and in April he flew from Cody to Denver and from Denver to Fort Worth. On the second leg of his flight he met up with J. C. Bonine, and they sat next to each other on the small propeller plane that skidded and bumped through the high winds out of Denver.

"You know, that's more money than either one of us has ever seen," Bill said to J.C., referring to the prize purse they would compete for the following day. "We ought to consider whichever one of us ever wins, we ought to split what we win."

J.C. considered Bill's suggestion quietly to himself but didn't seem too interested. He didn't agree to it, but he didn't disagree, and when they arrived in Fort Worth Bill suggested the plan to some of the others—Bud Munroe, Joe Marvel, Bill Pauley. He said they all ought to make a pool and split their winnings because that would assure all of them some money. The younger cowboys were quite confident they could win against the old cowboys, who, while talented, were winners of the past, and they politely declined Bill's offer. He thought they were being foolish and arrogant, but it was only a further indication of his aging. He was no longer the young superstar he had been, and however the younger generation respected him, they also now believed they could beat him. Later that night, J.C. came around and agreed with Bill to split the first place purse, if either of them should win it, fifty-fifty.

The match in Fort Worth worked on a pyramid structure: the sixteen cowboys drew lots to pair up for eight matches, and in each match a cowboy got two horses. The cowboy with the highest combined score in each match would move into the next round—this time eight cowboys pairing off for four matches, and so on. For his first match, Bill drew Jim Kelts, a very good, young bronc rider from Canada. Kelts was riding consistently better than Bill in the regular season, and he rode well in the match, but Bill rode better, just barely, and won. In the next round Bill drew Joe Marvel, his friend and the current world champion. Joe was one of three young bronc riding brothers known as "the Marvel Boys." Ten years Bill's junior, Joe reminded Bill of the young Jim Houston. The kid had an instinctive feel for a horse and the way it moved; like Jim, he was a natural. "Joe Marvel was one of the two or three best bronc riders I ever saw," Bill said almost thirty years later, "and just as nice a guy as there ever was." Joe's father, Tom, had been a bronc rider in his younger years and had raised his three boys in the saddle. The Marvels' door was always open to traveling cowboys, and Bill had stayed there several times. Before they drew their horses for the match contest, Bill had a feeling that he had no chance of beating Joe Marvel, who at that time was clearly the better rider. But Bill drew two great horses, and Joe drew two mediocre ones. "There is no way that I should have ever, in 1979, beat Joe Marvel in a bronc riding match," Bill said, but he did.

J.C. had also won his first match, advanced to the second round, and won. In the semifinals, J.C. and Bill drew each other. Bill got on his first horse and rode well, and J.C. missed his first horse out. Bill rode his second horse clean, and again J.C. failed to mark out. Although it wasn't terribly unusual for a cowboy to miss two horses out, it was unusual for J.C., which made it look as though J.C. hadn't ridden like he'd wanted to win. Perhaps Bill's deal with him had affected his ride. Either way, Bill's win left him facing Bud Munroe in the final round. Another young bronc rider ten years Bill's junior, Bud was a friend and traveling companion of Bill's brother Rick. Just looking at Bud reminded Bill of himself ten years earlier, before he had won his first world championship, back when he was on the brink of a breakthrough. In ten years Bill had won three world championships, driven hundreds of thousands of miles, wrecked a marriage, broken his back, recovered, met Carole, fallen in love. And here he was.

The yellow chute gate opened, and a sorrel horse lunged out with Bill aboard. Bill sat upright with his legs extended, his spurs locked in the horse's shoulders for almost a full second. He held the rope rein tightly in his left hand. His right hand swung up above his head as if he were waving to the crowd. As the horse landed, Bill's feet snapped back. His spurs traced an arc along the gelding's belly. From the announcer's booth, the legendary Bob Tallman commented on the ride: "Cody Bill is really strong with his feet! He makes it look so simple!" By the time Tallman could say two short sentences, Bill's time was up. The buzzer sounded. The pickup men came to retrieve him, and Tallman exclaimed, "There's probably the best ride of the week." The crowd was on its feet.

A video was taken of the entire competition, and the few minutes of Bill's rides have been worn thin in the VCR by his nephew, Reid. Though he will never be a bronc rider himself, Reid has watched his uncle's famous ride hundreds of times. On that ride, an article in the *Western Horseman* commented that "never in his career was his spurring lick more perfect. The Bill Smith style is still an aspiration for most of the others." The young Bud Munroe could not compete. It wasn't his time, not just yet. He would have his own breakthrough and win his own world champion buckle one day. But in that moment, for his last ride, Bill walked away with the crowd cheering, with a check for $18,500 that he would split with his friend J.C., and he would go home to his new life.

As Bill left the Fort Worth arena, Tallman questioned him over the PA: "How many more broncs are you gonna ride, Bill?"

Bill held his hand high, extending only his index finger. He had announced his retirement, and the press had picked it up and publicized the Copenhagen-Skoal as his last ride. But shortly before the Copenhagen-Skoal match, the Professional Rodeo Cowboys Association asked Bill if he would ride one more time, in July. The PRCA had built a museum to showcase the sport of rodeo and a Hall of Fame to honor its stars, and the PRCA board voted for Bill Smith to be one of the hall's original inductees. As part of the ceremony, they wanted to have one of the inductees in each event compete against the current world champion in a two-round match, similar to the final round of the Copenhagen-Skoal exhibition. Joe Alexander was the inductee in bareback riding, and he was to match Jack Ward; Harley Mae would bulldog against the old-timer Roy Duvall, and so on. In the saddle bronc riding, Bill would face Joe Marvel again. He had reluctantly agreed.

U

The opening of the PRCA Museum and Hall of Fame in Colorado Springs, Colorado, was scheduled for July of 1979. To be an original inductee was an honor, but Bill didn't think much of it at the time. Partly he was being modest, sincerely wondering how it came about that he was nominated at all. He felt there were plenty of other talented bronc riders who might have earned the nomination just as easily. Partly, the novelty of the new Hall of Fame diminished its significance for him, since it was impossible to know whether it would ever be taken seriously. And partly, his retirement still hadn't sunk in yet. Although he hadn't ridden a bronc since April, he hadn't been out of the game that long. Not enough time had passed for him to get nostalgic. And he still knew everyone—the judges, the competitors, the secretaries—so he felt like he was still a part of it. He might not have completely accepted that fact that he wasn't going to ride anymore. He still had his saddle.

The ProRodeo Hall of Fame sits just off I-25 north of Colorado Springs. Outside, as a symbol and a beacon, a life-size statue of Casey

Bill Smith on Descent at the National Finals Rodeo in Oklahoma City, 1971. Bill rode Descent nine times in his career and considered him the greatest bucking horse of all time. Photo by Bern Gregory. Courtesy of the National Cowboy and Western Heritage Museum, Oklahoma City.

Tibbs stands against the sky. Inside, plaques with the names of the world champions in each event hang on the walls, and photographs of great rides are displayed on panels in the middle of the room. Each of the inductees have a photograph displayed in a case, each in his or her location, grouped according to event. Some inductees donated equipment and memorabilia to be displayed in the cases; others kept their saddles, chaps, boots, belt buckles, and hats. Bill told the Hall of Fame that he would give them his gear, but before he could give it up he had to ride one last time.

"At that stage in my career, he was far better than I was," Bill said of his competition with Joe. "There was actually no way I could beat him if he didn't mess up." Bill's first horse out, Kinai News, earned him eighty-six points. He made a bold ride, spurring hard and totally in control. Joe rode the horse Jackson Hole, which, according to Bill, wasn't any good, and Joe's second ride on Miss Descent couldn't make up for his low-score ride on Jackson Hole. Bill rode the horse Stetson for eighty points and, for the last ride of his career, took the win. When he left the Hall of Fame, he gave his saddle and his chaps and all his equipment to be stored safely in an exhibit behind a sheet of glass. With this last ride, against a competitor half his age, the old-time champion hung up his spurs and left the arena open for the next crop of cowboys to walk into the limelight.

Later that year, Bill and Carole visited the museum together so that Carole, who had missed the induction, could see Bill's place in the museum and so that Bill could visit Descent. Alongside the cowboys, famous horses and bulls were awarded places in the ProRodeo Hall of Champions, and Descnet was among them. Since Bill's induction ceremony, Descent had been delivered to live out his days at the Hall of Fame's barn and pasture. By that time, Descent was an old horse and, like Bill, at the end of his career. It was said that the horse never let anyone touch him, and the museum staff told Bill that when people came to see Descent he would go to the other side of the pen. Bill said, "He'll recognize me for all the times he's bucked me off." And sure enough, when they leaned on the fencerail, Descent walked right up to meet Bill. The old buckskin approached the rail and stood stock still, and Bill reached out and gently stroked the great horse's nose.

Chapter 11

Into the Normal

In 1974, when Bill was struggling with his back injury and surgery, he got to thinking more and more about his life after rodeo. By the National Finals he was in terrible pain, he was slipping in the standings, and the fight was slowly seeping out of him. One night after the rodeo, when everyone gathered in a hotel room to drink and carouse and rehash the day, Bill went and found Joe Marvel's father, Tom, and said simply, "I want to learn how to ride."

Tom was flabbergasted.

"How can a world champion bronc rider want to ride better?"

"I can hang on for eight seconds, but that's not riding," Bill said.

The conversation was reminiscent of a story from Will James's book *Cowboys North and South* in which a silver-spurred champion bronc rider goes on a cattle drive with his cowboy friends and, after falling off his gentle horse several times in an hour, is forced to admit that he doesn't know how to ride. Only Bill had grown up riding, he rode for a living in the off-season, and, despite what he said, he knew plenty about horses. But when Bill said he wanted to understand horses the way Tom did, he wasn't talking about anything quantifiable.

Tom Marvel was a rodeo champion himself, retired for many years already, and was known to be a terrific horseman. Bill had stayed with the Marvels at their ranch on Battle Mountain several times while he was traveling the circuit, and on one occasion he watched Tom Marvel work with a crop of fresh two-year-old colts that had never been ridden before. Tom took the time to stand with a colt in the round pen until he could walk up and lay a hand on its back, and then a blanket, and finally a saddle. It was far faster to rope off one leg and tighten the cinches while the horse fought and tried to kick itself free, but, Tom explained, this gentle way just worked better.

Tom Marvel had learned much of what he knew from a cowboy who worked for him by the name of Tom Dorrance. Dorrance was an older guy with prominent features, no upper lip, and half a front tooth missing. His hands were several shades darker than the rest of him. He had been in Nevada, Oregon, Idaho, and California, and everywhere he went people seemed to learn something from him. He could work with any kind of horse, no matter how testy or difficult, and things would always come out well. For a time Dorrance had worked for Marvel on the 25 Ranch in Nevada. Over several years of working with him, Tom Marvel learned some things about working with horses that he passed on to his sons and anyone else who cared to listen. Neither Dorrance nor Marvel had a soapbox, exactly, but they had a kind of method, a kind of quiet philosophy about working with horses that seemed to meet with great success. They could ride any horse anywhere and teach it to do anything, and they could work with a horse with a harmony Bill had never seen before.

Being a good horseman was not like being a world champion bronc rider; there was no measure of greatness, no winner or cash prize. The work put into becoming a better horseman wouldn't necessarily pay off in any tangible way. It was a purely artistic pursuit, the way a painter paints because it is her passion, her desire, and her method of communication. And the fact that Bill wanted to learn this new method was a sign that something within him was changing—a sense of priority and a sense of perspective. Bill had always been willing to break from tradition or to be the odd one out, but this new method of dealing with horses required a person to be patient, to command not by force but by suggestion, to work in partnership and not as an individual. These were not his usual habits.

"There's a guy," Tom said, "by the name of Ray Hunt. He used to work with Tom Dorrance, and now he goes around putting on what he calls clinics. You should go look him up and go to one of his clinics and see if you like what's going on." Bill wrote the name Ray Hunt in the small spiral notebook he carried in his shirt pocket. Later that evening he told J.C. Bonine about the conversation he'd had with Tom Marvel, and J.C. said he would go with Bill to one of these clinics if Bill found out where there was one. Later that year, they took off from rodeoing for a weekend and they went together to meet Ray Hunt in Billings, Montana.

In 1974 rodeo still carried with it much of the reputation it had gained in the early days when cowboys would pull into town for a week or two and party the whole time like it was New Year's Eve. Bronc riders were thought to be cocky yahoos who were as likely to know nothing about horses as they were to be real ranch-raised hands, and when Bill and J.C. showed up at Ray Hunt's clinic, Ray Hunt was not particularly welcoming. In the 1970s Ray was still a young man, not much older than Bill, and his clinics were new territory for western horsemen. As Bill tells it, Ray was presenting a technique and a philosophy that ran counter to everything the old cowboys knew and held true. People challenged him all the time, but he wasn't interested in arguing. His lessons weren't required, and he wasn't telling anyone they had to do anything any certain way. He saw his clinics as presentations and practice sessions where he could show people how to work with their horse, but what they practiced on their own time was up to them. "You had to kind of convince him that you were sincere before he'd turn himself over to you," Bill said, and in fact at that first clinic Ray paid little attention to him. Despite the fact that he was not like most, Bill was still a bronc rider by name and by trade, and his status brought along with it the assumption that he was hardheaded and arrogant. The way Ray rode and thought about riding was just the opposite of what a bronc rider was known to do and be.

On the first day of the clinic, Ray sat on his horse in the middle of a wide arena, and his students gathered around him in a scattered semicircle. Most of the students were cowboys and working ranchers. Ray, having been raised on his father's farm, could relate to them. He was quiet and almost shy. He introduced himself and, as the group sat easy in their saddles and their horses lowered their heads with the reins draped loosely over their necks, told them the very beginning of his thoughts. "I've had different people ask me how long it takes to break a horse," he began. "Well, I never rode a broke horse, but then maybe I'm a sorry hand." The crowd chuckled, and a few horses shifted. One man's horse started to walk off, and he picked up the reins and circled him back around.

"I don't know what you have to offer your horse so that your horse can come through for you," Ray continued, "but the horse can do anything you ask of him. Some of them can do things better than others, but each one can do his thing his way as well as he can. For me, the horse doesn't have to do my thing my way, but I do want him to do my thing his way and like it. To me, we aren't teaching these horses to walk, trot, turn around, stop, or anything. They can do any of these things. What we are trying to teach them is to do these things when we ask them. This is the tough part, to get them to understand to do it when we ask. When we're not on his back he can run out there and stop, turn around, or whatever. When it's his idea it's simple for him. But his problem is to figure out what in the world we want at this particular instant—how much to move out at this time and how much to slow down. The easy way for me to show him is to be a part of him, be right close to him and move with him."

Ray wanted rider and horse to move as one being, so seamless that they would appear to be one animal the way American Indians had once thought the Spaniards and their horses were. His theory and his method were in fact nothing new; people had been training horses with this method for centuries, but somewhere in the history of the American cowboy it had gotten lost. On the frontier, horsemanship was not an art like it was for the Spaniards, the Indians, or the Mongols.

"To understand the horse, you'll find that you're going to be working on yourself," Ray went on. "As we go along, this is the way it is: we are responsible within ourselves for what happens. In your own mind you have to have a picture of what you want from the horse, but you are the leader and you can ask him to follow you, just like dancing." What he said echoed Casey Tibbs's comparison of bronc riding to dancing with a girl. The two weren't as much in opposition as it seemed. Perhaps that was the secret of the greatest bronc riders: that it was never a fight; it was a dance. Maybe it was the horse who led and the bronc rider who followed, or maybe the very good bronc rider could lead his horse.

"It's a rhythm, a harmony," Ray said. "You want your body and his body to become one. This is our goal. It takes some physical pressure naturally, to start with, but you keep doing less and less physical and more and more mental. Pretty soon it's just a feel following a feel, whether it comes today, tomorrow, or next year. So one little thing falls into line, into place. I wish it would all fall into place right now for you, but it doesn't because it has to become a way of life. It's a way you think. It's a way you live. You can't make any of this happen, but you can let it happen by working at it."

Ray continued, explaining his overall philosophy and end goals. Most of what he said seemed easy, and he presented his thoughts in a way that made perfect sense. He talked for a long time before instructing the class to move out to the edge of the arena. They spent most of the rest of the day walking and stopping, walking fast and walking slow, and sometimes standing completely still. Ray wanted each rider to know where each of his horse's feet were at every moment. He wanted them to know when each foot was lifting off the ground and being set back down. He wanted a cowboy to be able to halt his horse so the right front foot was the last to stop; to move the horse's front end to the left so the left front foot was the first to lift off the ground. Ray asked the class to make the most exacting moves—to take five steps forward, two steps back, take a quarter turn to the right with only the front feet, take a quarter turn to the left with only the back. "Think right down to the ground," Ray said. "In other words, your horse is an extension of your body. Whether we're speeding the horse up, slowing him down, stopping, or backing him, we're working for a feel between rider and horse—less physical and more mental contact all the time. The feet are in your hands."

In the afternoon, Ray talked as the class walked around and around. "A walk is a four-beat gait and should be regular. You should be able to control it. You are picking his feet up and setting them down. You're going with him so he can learn to go with you. It's feel, timing, and balance. It can become as natural as breathing." On the second day, the class collected around Ray and held their reins loosely waiting for instruction. Ray had a slow, cool voice, and he knew to be patient when presenting his lessons. For every exercise they tried, the people and the horses were both Ray's students. He had to assume that neither had worked in tandem quite like this before and that neither knew exactly what he wanted to achieve. It would have been one thing to have people familiar with the process working with green horses, or even horses who had the soft feel paired with inexperienced people. But the combination he had before him was the most delicate.

Ray asked the class to pick up their reins and pull them gently toward their thighs until they felt the horse's mouth pulling against them. They held the reins steady there, anchoring them against the saddle, until the horse bent his neck ever so slightly, just enough to stop pulling against the bit. There, when the mouth was soft in the hands of the rider, the most delicate communication was possible. The slightest tug of the rein between the pinky and the ring finger of the right hand would tell the horse to turn his head slightly to the right; a tug of two degrees with both hands and a seat deep in the saddle would call a halt; the same tug at a slightly different angle and with a touch of the leg would ask for steps backward.

It took some time before Bill felt what Ray was asking for—the point at which there is no tension, no pressure. His horse pulled against him, and he pulled back. The horse threw his head up and down or tucked his neck in so far that the reins fell slack between them. Confused and thinking he was being asked to step back, the horse moved backward. They made these incremental movements and missteps for almost an hour. And then, finally, Bill relaxed. The horse ducked his head and stood still, holding the bit like a piece of taffy. The horse collected beneath him felt weightless. It was like floating in a lake and looking up at the sky, like holding a girl for the first time. Ray had them practice the soft feel at a walk. They never moved much faster than that.

U

When Bill came home to Carole he told her about the things Ray Hunt had taught. Carole was intrigued by the method and excited by Bill's enthusiasm. Later that year, they went to a clinic together and watched Ray start a crop of two-year-old colts. It was the same way Bill had seen Tom Marvel work with the colts on the 25 Ranch. One by one he turned them this way and that with a flag and then with a rope and halter. By the second day of a colt's education, Ray would have a rider step gently into the saddle and ride the little colt around. It was hardly the wild horse chase of Bill's rodeo days. Ray could walk up to his green colts after two days and they would stand stock still and turn their heads toward him to be haltered.

Watching Ray was something like magic for Bill. He had mastered the other way—the traditional cowboy way of muscle and bravado. But what Ray Hunt had showed him turned everything he knew about working with horses upside down. And as Ray presented it, the cowboy's relationship with his horse was just the beginning. "Ray Hunt is responsible for a revolution in attitude," Bill said, "especially for the western people I know, in how they look at, treat, and think about their horses.

"I grew up in a rough, take charge, take charge by force, win or lose atmosphere, and it took Ray Hunt to turn that around for me. For most people it's easier because they can't ride if a horse bucks, or if the horse misbehaves, they get scared. I always could stay on no matter what they done, and was never smart enough to be afraid. Consequently, it was harder for me to learn this other way because it was easy for me to just get in a battle. And I enjoyed the battle.

"Most of the things I knew when I first went to Ray Hunt were just the opposite of what I should have been doing. I had to turn my whole life around, my whole way of thinking. He made a difference in my attitude and the way I think about life—not just horses, but life. He taught me to just be at peace with things, to see the good in things, not the trouble. With your horse, you just want him to be the best he can be. You're not looking at him as good or bad; he is what it is, and you appreciate him for what he is. Then you start appreciating people for what they are, not for what you want them to be. He's the reason that

I can appreciate my marriage, he's the reason I can ride out there on any horse I get on and enjoy it, and he's the reason that I can be at peace with everything I've done in my life because of the way he taught me to think about things. I always say that I wish I could have met him sooner, but then I think and I realize that it wouldn't have done me any good, because I wasn't ready to accept that. I had that other thing in me, that contest and that competition thing that I had to deal with, and I had a perfect outlet for it, and I exhausted it. And when I got done, I was ready to accept the other thing."

U

The work with Ray Hunt had started Bill thinking about life down the road. He wasn't nearly ready to retire yet, but he knew the time would come soon enough. That spring, Bill's brother-in-law Jim Fike posed a question: "Have you ever thought about raising bucking horses?" Fike looked serious, but Bill didn't know exactly where he was going with the question. It was Easter weekend 1975, and they were snowed in at Fike's place near Pavillion. Jim had married Bill's little sister Diane a few years back, but Bill had never gotten to know him until that weekend when he and Carole drove their truck off the road in a snowstorm and Jim had come to rescue them.

"I've thought about it a lot," Bill said.

"Well, I've got the grass," said Fike. "We'd just have to get some mares and some studs. I say we go in partners." Jim's mother, Kitty, was a full-blooded Cherokee; being half-blood gave Jim rights to tax-free land if he lived on the reservation, and the reservation was open range. There was a limit to how many cows you could run but no limit on how many horses. They could keep their costs low and sell their stock at the Miles City bucking horse sale in Montana.

Since its beginnings in the early 1960s, the Miles City sale had been a stunning success. It was the place to buy and sell rodeo prospect horses, and by the cold afternoon Jim proposed his idea to Bill, bucking horses had become a hot commodity. Unlike the first half of the century when there were plenty of wild horses to be had, years of breeding for a gentler horse, coupled with glue and meat factories depleting the wild horse population during the war, left only a scarce pool of good bucking stock by the 1970s. In the 1940s and 1950s, a good bucking horse was ridden only ten or fifteen times a year, but by the 1970s the few good horses left were bucked an average of forty to fifty times a year. Even the best broncs were getting worn out, and cowboys were getting tired of drawing the same stock over and over again.

When he was a boy, in the days when he would drive anywhere there was a wild horse to get on, Bill went to Miles City every year. The Miles City sale was unique in that it was the only time a cowboy didn't have to pay an entry fee to ride but was instead guaranteed $5 a head for every horse he rode regardless of whether he made the whistle. It was also a notorious place to party. Miles City was one of the few towns in the West where prostitution was legal, and the bucking horse sale weekend was a boon for the infamous cathouses (or perhaps it was the cathouses that lured the horse buyers). A typical client for the madam was the cowboy who came straight from the rodeo grounds, slapped his winnings on the table in front of her, and declared, "Just tell me when I run out." In one brothel, signed pictures of world champion cowboys adorned the walls — a mark of the distinguished clientele — which, it was said in later years, included a picture of Bill.

With nothing to lose, Bill agreed to Jim's deal. Raising horses was something he had always wanted to do, and the extra cash from the sale of the horses would be nice to have. Together they rounded up thirty or forty mares, and Bill purchased a Percheron stallion from Tom Marvel. Within two years they had twenty or thirty offspring that they took to Miles City and sold. Their first horse out of the auction gate ran clear across the arena, ran into the far gate, broke her neck, and dropped dead. The same thing happened the next year and the next. Of the horses that died, they got more out of the insurance than the horse would have brought at auction. Of the others, they sold enough every year to make at least enough money to get home. After three or four years, Bill and Jim got the reputation of having the wildest horses around.

Although Bill believed in raising horses to buck, it was a bittersweet endeavor. As he got older, it was becoming more and more dangerous for him to tangle with the broncs, and it made him sad—nostalgic and at the same time aware of his own aging—to be around horses he knew he would soon be unable to ride. As he neared retirement, he and Carole talked about raising a crop of ranch horses. With gentle horses he could employ Ray Hunt's method of training and teaching, and he could continue to ride for many more years. "I knew I wanted to raise gray horses," Bill said, having always thought they were the prettiest. As he started talking to people, he heard about a horse with a good bloodline called Jackie Bee that was owned by a man named Duane Walker in Canton, Kansas. Bill tried to call the Walker ranch, but the only person he ever got to answer was a hired hand who said Mr. Walker was not home and had no interest in selling Jackie Bee.

Unsatisfied, Bill hitched up his trailer and took his brother Rick and drove to Kansas. They looked at a few other horses in the area and asked around about Jackie Bee. Everyone knew the horse and agreed the bloodline was the best, so Bill found Duane Walker's house and pulled into the yard. A tall, dignified-looking gentleman came out of the house and stood on the front porch waiting to see who had arrived. And as soon as Bill stepped out of the car, Walker approached, stuck out his hand, introduced himself, and said, "I've watched every ride you ever made at the Finals." Walker was honored to do business with Bill. Though he wasn't willing to sell Jackie Bee, he said Bill could breed Jackie Bee and get a good colt with nice color, and Bill could stand that stud. The order would take at least a year.

In the meantime, in the spring of 1979, two businessmen from Cody approached Bill with another idea. Lyle Ellis was a rodeo announcer who had met Bill during his early days at the Cody Night Rodeo. They had gotten to be friends during that time, and after Bill left town to make a name for himself, Lyle had followed his career with interest. When Lyle heard that Bill was retiring, he suggested to his business partner, Dick Curtis, with whom he had run the C&E Rodeo Corporation and later the Cody Night Rodeo, that the three of them produce a rodeo in North Platte, Nebraska. Each of the three would bring experience to the production, and Bill had a good deal of name recognition. In addition, Bill had horses. They could use the bucking horses he and Jim had been raising as the stock for their own rodeo.

Although North Platte, Nebraska, was not Carole's first choice of summer vacation spots, she was supportive of Bill's idea to start a rodeo of his own, and she agreed to be the rodeo secretary. When the school year was over, they packed their things and headed southeast. The three business partners borrowed $90,000 from two banks at a 21 percent interest rate, and they trucked the forty oldest colts from Bill and Jim's herd to the rodeo arena. They hired family and friends to judge, pick up, and run the chutes. They hung posters all over town. At the beginning of the summer they all had high hopes, but halfway through the first season the rodeo hadn't made any money.

The birthplace of Buffalo Bill, North Platte, Nebraska, is a place only because it is on the way to other places. Two hundred miles directly east of Cheyenne and 250 miles northeast of Denver, cowboys passed through town all summer long, and the motels were full of families by six or seven o'clock in the evening. But the grandstands remained empty. Bill couldn't understand why, if the motels were full, people weren't coming out for the rodeo, except to think that this simply wasn't their destination and was, therefore, not a place they were thinking about entertainment. They rolled in after a long day of driving and planned to be up and out as early as possible the next morning. To get them out of their hotel rooms once they were bunked down for the night was seemingly impossible.

Cowboys entered the rodeo nonetheless, and every evening after the rodeo Bill would organize a football game—the same kind of carefree fun he had enjoyed in his traveling days. The Smiths would play the visiting riders or whoever was around. Bill would be the quarterback throwing his wounded ducks. But for all the good times, and for all the clever strategic plays on the football field, the financials of the rodeo never worked in Bill's favor. By the middle of the summer, Carole was ready to leave. The rodeo wasn't making any money; it was a constant struggle, and being in the office all day reminded her of being in the classroom. She liked to spend her free time out of doors. Being a secretary, Carole said, "it just wasn't my thing." She stayed in

North Platte until the end of the season and returned to her teaching job in the fall. By the middle of the year, Dick and Lyle wanted to quit. Bill, certain he could make it work, assumed the loan from the bank, and Jim Fike agreed to help him.

As they were closing the books for the summer, a couple of stock contractors from the PRCA came and bought Bill and Jim's thirty best horses to use on the professional rodeo circuit. The profits from the sale were enough to cover the bills at North Platte for the year. And the sale was a testament to Bill and Jim's being in the right place at the right time, at least as far as the broncs were concerned. As for the rodeo, they put on seventy performances a summer for the next ten years. They advertised everywhere, put billboards on the interstate, and went to meetings and horse shows to promote themselves, but nothing worked. They never could get enough people to buy tickets to their rodeo. Only the sale of their bucking horses at the end of every year kept them solvent.

Bill was determined to turn this chapter, like most every other of his life, into a success story. "I thought if I kept going and stuck to it and tried hard enough I could make it work," he said. "We had a very good rodeo; we had good contestants. We had good performances and nice stock. We had a good thing going. We just couldn't get people to stop."

U

At the end of the first summer in North Platte, Bill called Duane Walker. Duane had a production sale in the first part of November every year where he sold about 120 colts at a higher price than anyone around. It was one of the big events of the quarter horse business, and Bill figured he could learn something from it if Duane needed an extra hand, which he did. Early in the fall, Bill went to Kansas and worked on Duane's sale. The horse sale business was something Bill knew nothing about, and just by being there he learned how to get horses ready for a sale and how to package and market them for auction.

The following year Duane rang up Bill. A couple who had bought a filly the year before had called to say that the two-year-old was a killer and an outlaw and that she'd hurt several people. They were disappointed with her, and they wanted Duane to do something about it or give them their money back. Duane asked if Bill would take the filly and ride her, and although Bill was busy with the rodeo in North Platte, he agreed to do this favor for his friend. Bill said that if Duane wanted to send the filly to North Platte, he'd see what she was like.

"So the people brought this pretty, young thing," Bill said. "Her tail was all wrapped so that she wouldn't switch it out, and just as fat as a pound dog. They wrote me a letter that said, 'Now you be careful. This mare is dangerous; she's hurt several people. Don't take any chances with her.' And I'd dealt with that line of horses, and I couldn't believe it. I put her in a pen, and I saddled her up, and she was fine. Just a saddle, I didn't put anything on her head. I had a little, short flag I used to guide her this way and that. I could see she was a little bit afraid.

"We had about a twenty-acre pasture right outside of that corral, and I just opened the gate on her. I didn't have anything on her head at all, just my saddle and a little flag. When she took out of there she throwed her head and started to stampede, and when she did I just started petting her. She loped out there about fifty or a hundred yards and just stopped and looked around and breathed a little sigh of relief seeing I wasn't going to get after her, and from that day on she was mine."

Two weeks later, Duane came to North Platte to see the filly, and Bill showed him what she could do. At the time, Duane was trying to get Ray Hunt to come and do a clinic in Canton, but after seeing Bill work with the filly he said that from the looks of the mare he would hire Bill.

U

On the morning of his first day in Kansas, Bill sat in the middle of a small round pen on his favorite gray horse. He was slightly nervous—not afraid so much as apprehensive. He had never thought of himself as a teacher, even though he'd helped a few bronc riders get on their way by bolstering their attitude and determination. Working with a horse—with people and their horses—was going to require putting actions, feelings, and philosophy into words. The round pen suddenly felt very small. The crowd—mostly young cowboys willing to get on never-before-ridden colts—stood around the rails sipping coffee from Styrofoam cups waiting for Bill to speak.

"First and foremost, everything that I know that works good I learned from Ray Hunt," he began. Years later, he would amend this remark to "First and foremost, everything that I know that works good I learned from Ray Hunt. But I've been around horses for almost sixty years now, and by accident you learn some things that work for you by just being around." He paused after this first sentence, and the people waited. It was early in the morning, early in the spring, and cold. Steam was rising from the coffee cups and exhalations.

"Well, let's get started," he said. "I want to start by saying I'm not a man of many words, and I don't speak so that everyone understands me. I spend my days with the horses, and I am constantly working to communicate better with the horse. Just think for a minute how badly we treat this animal. This here is a wild animal whose first instinct is flight. He's used to the open land, no fences, no stables. We take him and put him in prison in corrals, in stalls with bars. We put metal in his mouth and leather straps on his head and back. We've taken away his freedom. There are only two things in this world that I'd fight to the death for—the first is my wife. The second is my freedom. And here I've taken away this animal's freedom. So I want to make it the best I can for him."

The cowboys nodded in agreement. Bill was surprised at the reception and didn't know if the crowd was listening to him because a shift in attitude had already happened in Kansas or because he was a champion bronc rider and people assumed he knew something that he didn't. Either way, he seemed to have their attention. The colts pawed and kicked at one another and ran nervously up and down the alley leading to the round pen. He began by taking them one by one into the pen and running them in circles until they would stop and start and turn to him when he asked. Next he had all the colts brought into the round pen together. One by one, each cowboy got near enough to a colt that he could touch it, stroke its neck, loop a halter over its nose and ears, and tie it off. By noon ten cowboys held ten colts by strings. They draped the lead lines over the colts' backs and turned them by tugging gently on their halters. Finally, they put saddle blankets on their backs and saddled them, just letting the colts get used to the saddles. The next day the process would be repeated, but faster, and the cowboys would get on the colts for the first time. The third day, the same thing, and then they would ride out into an open field, the colts getting used to the feel of a rider on their backs, to the feel of a halter and a rope and of being directed by the nose. After the fourth day the colts would be turned out to pasture, not to be ridden again for another year while their bones and bodies grew.

In the afternoons, Bill worked with the people on grown and gentled horses the way he had learned with Ray Hunt. Carole had made nametags for all the participants with their names in bold, black letters so that Bill could read them from far away, and he started by asking people questions to get them involved. "Why do you ride?" he asked one cowboy. "What do you want to be able to do with your horse?" he asked another. "Which foot is your horse resting his weight on right now?" he asked a woman. As they stood standing in a circle around him, Bill explained the soft feel just like Ray Hunt had explained it to him but in his own words. He watched as the people pulled at the reins and shifted in their saddles trying to get the right combination of energy, attention, and calm, collected authority. Bill watched them individually, the people and their horses, and he could tell by watching the horses mostly—their muscles and reactions—what the people were doing wrong. As he watched one student after another, he started to see patterns in the way people moved and compensated and made mistakes. He was able to see how the horse responded, and he formulated as he watched these trials and errors, these series of reactions, how to think like the horse and to communicate those thoughts to his students. Over time he became a kind of interpreter, and one by one his students had their moments of epiphany.

Bill looked to Carole to help him be a better teacher and in turn developed a deeper respect for her. "Teaching is the hardest thing I ever tried to do," he said. "By doing these clinics, I really learned to have respect for teachers. It doesn't matter what you know; it doesn't matter at all. If you can't teach it and communicate it to other people, it doesn't do anybody any good. You just die and it's gone. Whatever horsemanship any of us have, if we can't teach it to other people it's not that much.

"What we do with the horses they will never forget. They have the dangdest memories. They will remember that for fifteen years, the rest of their lives. I liken it to a computer — once you put something in there, it's in there; you just have to push the right buttons to get it out. If the people don't learn what buttons to push, then it's their fault. What we teach the horses, and the reason it works, is the most natural thing for them. People are always saying, 'My horse won't do this,' but it's because they haven't taught him. If you teach him, if you present it to him so he understands — you know horses don't speak English or French or whatever — you've got to tell him so he'll understand, and then he'll do it.

"If it doesn't work out between a person and a horse, that's the person's fault. It's not the horse's fault; he didn't ask to be there. You are asking him to do something for you, and you have to respect him where he's at. And that doesn't mean where he's at today is where he was at yesterday or where he's going to be tomorrow. He can be fresh and fractious, but you've got to ride him where he's at, at that moment. Since I learned that, I've never had trouble with a horse. In fact, I've had a lot less trouble in general. It's like that with most things. If people can just slow down and relax and take things where they're at, they'd have a lot less problems.

"People are always trying to dominate. We're a dominating species, but we've just gotten too serious; we take ourselves way too seriously. In the end, man won't destroy the earth; man will destroy man. The earth will still be here long after man is gone. Mother Nature's got it all figured out. She has her way of making things right. Might take a hurricane or a flood, but she'll put it back the way she wants it. But people still go stickin' their nose in things, tryin' to fix things but mostly just destroyin'. More people should just relax and thank

Mother Nature that we're here, thank her for every second of it that she allows us to be here at all. We're just goddang lucky to be here. Most people don't realize that until they're too old to do anything about it; they're too busy tryin' to fix and run and dominate people, creatures, Mother Nature. They should just do what's right and kind, try to give the next guy a break—and not just the next guy but the next creature—and just be thankful to be here. People should just be more like the horse."

Chapter 12

Some Horses

For three years after she married and for five years before that, Carole lived in an eight-foot-wide trailer in Cody. When Bill was on the road or off in the mountains, it was just enough room for her; but when he was home, the trailer was tight for two. She wanted to move somewhere she could have space around her, someplace she could have horses.

In 1982 Sylvia Livingston made her an offer. Sylvia taught with Carole in Cody, and over the years the two had become friends. In 1966 Sylvia had inherited her grandmother's ranch in Thermopolis, and since that time she had let the land sit untouched. She hadn't bothered to lease it, nor had she thought to sell it, but every so often she drove out to make sure no one was squatting there and that everything was in order. The spring of that year, when the snows had melted out of the hills, Sylvia asked Carole to drive with her.

They drove east, up through the town of Meeteetsee, along a straight road across empty space. Besides the town, they saw nothing but scrub and sky for 120 miles in every direction clear to the horizon. Fifty miles after Meeteetsee the land turned red—a deep, hot, dry red like the surface of Mars. The hills were speckled with prickly pear and sage, and the old, red, iron-rich soil of the Triassic period appeared as raw gashes in the bland Jurassic rock. In places, the colors appeared in reverse-chronological order, as if the land were a multicolored layer cake that had been turned upside-down. When the mountains formed, the land twisted, buckled, jackknifed, and turned in geologic episodes unique to this area alone. Sylvia, a geologist, said, "Much of what you see was formed from violence." Carole liked listening to Sylvia talk about the land from a scientific perspective. She liked to know about the natural world, and especially about Wyoming, about the things that could be seen, so that she could teach her students. Sylvia was a good teacher herself, and she was easy to talk to. At least, it was easy to get her talking.

Sylvia turned right at the river and drove through town. A few minutes later she turned left, crossed the Bighorn River, stopped before a set of railroad tracks, and looked in both directions for the train. On the other side of the tracks, a narrow road was cut into the side of a steep hill. They followed the road for a mile and stopped by a dilapidated shack. "My grandfather started his law practice here in 1912," Sylvia said as they climbed out of her truck. "And he bought this chunk of land to live on. The only access was a cable that ran across the river, that you got in a little bucket and you did this." She pulled one hand over the other above her head. "So my grandfather and my father dynamited that road." Carole looked back toward the road they had come over, to the hills in the distance and the curve of the river that formed the eastern edge of the property line. It was a barren piece of land far, far away from anything. They were just slightly north of the exact center of Wyoming, and this was just what Carole liked—space, quiet. On the far side of the river, the land of the Arapaho reservation inclined toward the sky; to the north, a red mesa puckered up to the clouds. She took it in quietly.

"My grandfather died out here," Sylvia went on. "It was a terrible winter. I was little, so I don't remember, but he was drilling a hole in the ice with an ice auger. He was trying to open up a place for the cows because they were dying. My dad found him two hours later, froze, gone." It was hard to imagine, on such a beautiful day, that someone had frozen to death here. Sylvia continued, "So the other day my father said to me, 'Sylvia, the bums are going to burn that house down. If I were you, I'd go burn it myself. If you don't do it, it's just going to burn everything when it catches. And fire trucks just don't come over that hill.' So, look at this," she said, waving an arm out to encompass all the land before her. "I've got to do something, Carole. I've got to find someone to burn the house down. I've got to do something with my land."

Carole looked at the house and beyond to the cottonwood trees that grew along the river. From the river, Sylvia's two hundred acres rose gently from flat pastures to sheltering hills.

"This is beautiful," Carole said.

The next day, Carole and Bill found Sylvia at home in Cody. She invited them in and offered them a cup of coffee.

"How'd you like to lease that land?" Bill said. "We want to try to raise some horses."

Sylvia knew that Bill and Carole didn't have any money, certainly not enough to buy and barely enough to lease her two hundred acres, but she wasn't going to live there herself. Besides the railroad bums who knew they could drag mattresses into the old house and stay all night, no one had lived there for fifty years. She named a price far lower than what she thought she could have gotten had she leased the land to a hunting outfitter or sold it to the oil companies. She didn't like the former, and she hated the latter. Sylvia wanted the land to be used, as it had been by her family, to homestead. She loved the idea of a herd of horses grazing in the fields.

Sylvia's one stipulation was that the old house be burned down, and Bill and Carole agreed to this. But the week after they'd made the deal, Bill and Carole moved in. They had to sell Carole's trailer to finance the deal. There was no money left over to build a new house or rent a new trailer. They needed that money to buy irrigation pipes and to fence the pastures, and eventually to buy horses. The filthy shack, with its newspaper insulation and bare light bulbs, would have to do.

"Carole's mother and my mother were so disgusted when they thought I was going to ask her to live in that place," Bill said. "It was painted every color of the rainbow. We remodeled it and disinfected it the best we could; we paneled it with some old, cheap paneling and made it livable. We heated that house with one coal stove. There were four-inch gaps in the bottoms and tops of all the doors. But it didn't leak; that's the one thing it didn't do."

Bill and Carole Smith in the shack in Thermopolis, Wyoming. Collection of Bill Smith.

Surrounding the house there was virtually nothing but land and sky in every direction, and that sustained Carole for seven years. The road that Sylvia's father and grandfather had blasted was not negotiable without four-wheel drive, and for the first year or two Carole walked the long road and the steep hill, over the railroad tracks to school. "Whether it was twenty below zero or ninety above, she walked out of here," Bill remembered. And she was happy. In the evenings, when they sat together and imagined the future, they saw a herd of horses grazing along the bend of the Bighorn River. Grays, buckskins, blacks, sorrels, and bays ran together, their necks and backs moving like waves.

U

By the fall of 1982, when the geese heading south were stopping to rest in the brambles by the river, Bill and Carole had collected ten or twelve mares and a stud that Bill had bought from Duane Walker. The stud, Tee Jay Three Bars, was a Jackie Bee stallion, a muscular gray with a gentle disposition; the mares were all quarter horses, and mostly grays, Bill's favorite color. Like most cowboys, Bill favored the quarter horse for its speed, strength, and character. Their mix of blood combined the sturdiness of the mustang with the speed of the thoroughbred for an ideal combination of looks and speed—a deep-bodied, muscular, alert, and cooperative horse. A relatively new breed, officially recognized with the formation of the American Quarter Horse Association in 1940, they had quickly become the most popular horses in the West. Bill's idea was to breed, raise, and train a batch every year and sell them in the spring at an auction like Duane Walker's. He told his friends and family, trying to get them involved, but to his surprise no one wanted a part in it. The popular consensus was that no one looking for a gentle ranch horse would look to buy from an old rodeo cowboy.

Bill saw it another way. He trusted in his own ability to select good horses and in his and Carole's ability to make them sound. With the horses he and Carole already had, it wouldn't cost them much to breed the mares. Carole was teaching full-time, which provided at least one steady income, and Bill would work as an outfitter in the interim. They figured they had nothing to lose. "We started like we started everything else," Bill said later, "with zero." Though there was probably more to lose than they admitted at the time, the old attitude was there: the only way to come out on top is to go in believing that you will succeed.

That spring they put the twelve mares out to pasture with their stud. Eleven months later, in the spring of 1983, the mares dropped their foals, and it was a good crop. But even with a good set of colts, people would not come to a sale to bid on only a handful of horses. Bill figured they needed at least forty horses to make an auction worth anyone's while. In the fall, he hitched a trailer to his truck and left Thermopolis to find them. That winter he spent what little money they had left and collected a small herd—forty-seven horses total, including the babies who, on January 1, all turned one year old and in accordance with breeding laws were then considered weaned yearlings. Bill called six of his old rodeo friends to work the sale. Finally, knowing a good auctioneer would make a difference, he got a hold of Jack Campbell, one of the foremost auctioneers at the time. He called Jack and said, "This is Bill Smith, Cody Bill," and Jack knew Bill's rodeo name right away. "It's the only reason we got him to come be our auctioneer," Bill said later. Together they picked a sale date, May 12, 1984. Everything was falling into line—the horses, the hands, the auctioneer. But Bill and Carole didn't have grocery money to feed the crew.

Bill had grown much more confident in his abilities as a horseman since his success with Duane Walker's colts, and Carole suggested he run a clinic in Thermopolis to scrape together grocery money. They put out some advertisements and posted flyers around town for a three-day colt starting clinic. For $50, the flyer advertised, a person could have Bill Smith help them bridle, saddle, and ride their horse for the first time—and, to Bill's surprise, people went for it. He had sixteen colts in his first class, and the clinic cleared $800, which bought ample groceries for the sale crew. "That's kind of the way we operated back then," Bill said.

A few weeks later the crew showed up, grateful for the work, and parked their trailers beside Bill's shack. They washed and groomed all the horses the night before the auction and stabled them at the fairgrounds. They set up bleachers around the auction ring and rode the horses around one by one as Jack Campbell spun the numbers until each lot sold. People who were there said that most of the forty-seven horses at that first sale were "broncy sons of guns," real cowboy horses. Nonetheless, they sold. The average price was $2,500, some colts selling for $400 and some older geldings for over $4,000. Especially exciting for Bill was the surprisingly high average for the colts, the horses he had raised.

"That was a heck of a sale," Carole said later. "We didn't have a lot in it—we didn't have a lot of advertising, a lot of expense in it. We thought, boy, this is too easy." Bill thought of it in terms of his lifelong luck. "By today's standards it wasn't anything," he said modestly, "just a bunch of old bronc riders starting something that worked real good."

Carole continued teaching, and Bill spent another summer in North Platte, and they planned a second annual sale for the following spring. Things continued in this manner for a number of years. Carole was transferred from Cody to the school in Lucerne, seven miles outside of Thermopolis. Still without four-wheel drive whenever Bill had the truck, she adopted a new procedure for getting to school: she rode her horse into town and exchanged him at the veterinarian's clinic for her car, which she left in the parking lot, drove the seven miles to school, and returned to her horse at the end of the day. In the mornings and in the evenings, before she left and when she returned to the ranch, she moved the irrigation pipes, each about thirty feet long and forty pounds without water, across the fields. When she had time, she went riding in the hills. Meanwhile, Bill zigzagged his way across the country with his empty trailer. When the trailer was full he would return to Thermopolis, deliver the horses, and head out again. When he was home, he and Carole rode together in the hills behind the house, where the soil is blood red and ochre. In the summers, Bill went to North Platte alone, while Carole, who resigned from her position as rodeo secretary, rode her horses full-time.

Years later, Bill would reflect on his life with Carole, remembering especially these early days. "Carole is the mainstay of everything I've done, and she has been since 1974," he said. "When she was home in the middle of the winter and I was in Texas and I needed somebody to get into one of them old, rickety trucks with bad tires and a trailer in and go to Canada and get a load of mares, she'd do it. She'd be up there stuck and figure out how to get another tire, and we never had any money, and she never complained. She acted like it was a privilege for her to be able to do that. It's hard to express what a good woman that is. And she's been through the fire; I've tested her. One thing I did for her: I always loved her, and I always was faithful to her. I misused her and I overworked her, but I always loved her and I always was faithful to her. To this day she gives three times more than she gets."

U

In 1989 Bill spent his last summer in North Platte. The rodeo had never achieved the level of success he had hoped for, and the sale now occupied most of his time, interest, and energy. "I was determined," he said later of the North Platte years. "We put on I think seventy some performances a summer there for ten years. Each year we would sign a contract with the rodeo committee — just a bunch of town people that were trying to promote rodeo — but they never could pay us. When we left there they owed us some $60,000 that they just didn't have. So we just left. But before we left there we paid that bank back in full.

"That was one of the real disappointments of my life. I wish I could have done better with it, but I didn't. I hung in there until I almost sunk everybody. When I finally gave up and came home and put my energy into this sale and the clinics, that's when things started to turn around; that's when things started working for me."

Through the 1990s the sale got bigger and more successful with every year. Bill was making contacts with people across the country and horse sellers and agents were beginning to know his name. People became accustomed to what Bill Smith liked in a horse, which was the only kind of horse he wanted to buy and the only kind of horse he would sell: a middle-of-the-road, all-around quarter horse between four and eight years old, bred more for performance than speed, with eye-appeal, soundness, and a good disposition.

"I like them to be good-looking horses," he said after many years of selection experience. "I try not to get blemishes. I spend a little time with them, ride them, watch them being ridden. There are just little senses you can tell, see how they react to certain things. And I usually try to know who I'm buying from. What I look for is what you see there in the corral. Them horses were all brought here because they all had the potential to be good horses. I'll go anywhere to look at a horse, anywhere in the United States." Over the years he developed a network of traders who would call him whenever they found something he might like. "They're doing it because they know I'll give them a little bit more for one if they get one I like," he explained. "I've cultivated and worked on that little network ever since I began because I've got to have satellites out there in order to get exposed to all the horses I need."

As the quality of the horses increased, the sale prices increased; and as the profits from the sale increased, Bill was able to purchase a better product. Satisfied customers and ranch owners started buying horses in volume—three or four or five horses, as many as seven at one sale—and business started to take off. Soon the volume buyers began bidding wars, and the sale prices skyrocketed. Word spread that the WYO Quarter Horse Ranch sale was the place to buy quarter horses, and people started coming from all around. The average price of a WYO horse rose steadily—from $4,382 in 1997 (more than the high-selling horse in 1984) to $5,500 in 1998 to $5,731 in 1999, with many good horses selling for $12,000–$20,000. In 2000 the average jumped to $7,381 thanks to the sale of one gray gelding to a gentleman from Maryland. The horse belonged to Bill's brother Rick, who parted with him sadly and declared, "I'd rather have the horse than the money," but he let the horse go, nonetheless. The gelding sold for $81,000.

In the fall of 2000, Bill and Carole received an e-mail request for a sale catalog. It read:

> Hello Bill and Carole,
> I'm living in Littleton, Colorado, currently, but I grew up in the same area as you did Bill. . . . My dad (Joe Israel) worked at the Bearcreek school and always liked to tell the story of you and your brother playing hooky, usually you were off riding when school was in session. Said he told you you'd never make a living riding horses. Always said, with a laugh, that you proved him wrong. My dad died in '91, but I'll always remember that story.
> I recently heard of the big sale of your gray gelding—news spread all the way down here. Don't know if I can afford any of your horses since that happened, but thought I'd write for a sale catalog anyway.
> Jan Craig
> Sept. 6, 2000

With the success of the sale, Bill had made a new name for himself. As much as he was a former rodeo star, he was a horse trainer, a good hand, a horseman.

Bill Smith at one of his clinics, Chugwater, Wyoming, 2002. Photo by Margot Kahn.

U

Toward the end of May, people haul empty trailers from Florida, Vermont, Massachusetts, New Mexico, North Carolina, Canada, California, Montana, and West Virginia to Thermopolis, Wyoming. They bring their trailers empty, and they come ready to bid; some leave with seven horses, and some leave towing the same light trailer home.

The night before the sale there is a get-together where prospective buyers can sit and watch video footage of the horses working and roping. They sit in folding chairs in the fair building and watch the televisions as Bill's nephew Jack Wipplinger calls out the lot numbers. Bill sits with his mother in the kitchen. Everyone has been working all day, every day for months—riding, watering, feeding, blanketing—and the adrenaline is pumping on Friday night. Bill's niece Lori Coy greets people at the door; Rick Smith chats with buyers; Carole munches carrots and green peppers and chats with friends. Everyone is dolled up and decked out, clean and shaven, wearing pressed shirts and shined boots. Mel Hyland is smiling. All the hands are tan and tired, scrubbed but still gritty and burnt from forehead to collar.

While the prospective buyers watch the video, part of the crew heads out behind the fair building to the stables. The horses must be numbered and watered and fed. Family and friends carry the branding numbers and cans of paint, walking up and down the rows of stalls and numbering flanks—white paint for the blacks, sorrels, roans, dark grays, palominos, and the grulla; black paint for the light grays and buckskins. Each is haltered and led to water; each is tossed his allotment of alfalfa. Prospective buyers wander out of the fair building and linger. Two ladies gaze adoringly at the little palomino; a gentleman waits patiently for lot 17 to be led out, watching to see how he moves. The people ask questions: Is he smooth? Is he gentle? Does he work cows? Is he finicky about his head? They ask which horses to look at for their wives, girlfriends, children. One man asks if he can measure a horse to be sure it's not over fifteen hands; his wife is petite, he says, and she needs a small horse. The cowboys ask questions of the buyers, trying to gauge their experience, trying to fit the horses they know intimately with a person they know hardly at all.

The feeding and watering carries on until 10 P.M., then all hands head to bed. The crew meets again at 5:30 A.M. for breakfast at the Sideboard, the café everyone calls "Bill's office." Normally he goes alone to have coffee with the neighboring ranchers, but this morning the waitresses are prepared for Bill and his crew to fill the brown-and-tan diner. There isn't much chit-chat today; there are last-minute instructions, reminders, and a quick meal. From there it's back to the fairgrounds where the preview horses are led out, watered, unbraided, and brushed. They are rubbed with smooth cloths soaked in water and soap and oil until they shine. They are saddled and warmed up. The steers are sent through the chute and given shots of Ace, dressed with head guards, and sent out into the arena with the ropers. The arena dirt is dry and rises in clouds of red dust beneath the spotlights. Buyers filter into the grandstand. The sky is cloudless. The land needs rain, but not today.

The preview takes two hours. The horses must be rewashed and watered. The buyers make their final rounds, returning to their favorite stalls, asking more questions, rereading their sale books and dog-earring pages. At noon, the first colts are brought out to be groomed. They have been kept blanketed, and their coats are soft as velvet. Their tails are wrapped, coats reshined, hooves blackened, manes and forelocks oiled and gelled, muzzles glittered, ears cleaned with linseed oil and alcohol, nostrils wiped. They must stand patiently, without kicking dust or rubbing their legs or touching their noses to the ground, for nearly an hour, waiting for their numbers to be called.

When Bill welcomes the crowd, the action begins. The colts are led out by Carole; the broke horses are ridden by Mel Hyland, Rick Smith, Jack Wipplinger, and others. Behind the auction ring, horses are saddled and loped in circles to warm up; when their numbers are called they are ridden into the round pen, walked, trotted, cantered, turned, stopped, backed. They are asked to move one foot at a time, as they have been taught, to pivot gently with the slightest, almost unseen pressure—the tap of a spur—applied to their side. Jim Fike watches one section of bidders raising their hands or fingers. The more experienced nod their heads or blink their eyes; he knows to watch these certain people for their slightest movement, their barely perceptible suggestion. Like a master magician, he knows the secret of how to get his section bidding. On the far side of the auction ring, Edna sells hot dogs and soda.

It takes six hours to auction one hundred head of horses. Around three o'clock a young girl, maybe ten years old, buys her first horse. Bill stops the sale to watch the smile spread across her face. Carole goes and shakes her hand and congratulates her. The girl has no idea that Carole is a champion barrel racer, that Carole could be her hero. At that moment, the girl can only think of the beautiful gray horse she will ride and call her own. Tall and slim and elegant, Carole is beaming, radiant. She understands completely.

♘

The next morning everyone is at the Sideboard again, early. The women have the money and are going to the bank at ten o'clock, but people still need to be paid before they hit the road, and a storm is

Bill and Carole Smith, 2006. Photo by Holly Clanahan. Courtesy of *America's Horse*.

coming in. Bill sits with Jim and Todd Fike. They discuss the averages, the money, more logistics: who is going to drive the truck to Rock Springs, who is going to haul horses from Pavillion, Wyoming, who has been working especially hard and has a long drive and deserves to go home early.

"Next year," says Jim, beginning to shoot off ideas for how to do things differently, how to make things better, "I can't wait for next

year!" he says excitedly. His eyes are flashing and he sits forward, ready
to say more. For all of Jim's energy, Bill is exhausted. His elbows rest
on the table as he rubs his eyes and temples. "I don't even want to
think about next year," he says. All the energy of yesterday, of the past
months, is drained. In this one, rare moment, Bill looks much older
than his sixty years.

"But you were great," Bill, lifting his head, says earnestly to Jim.
"Better this year than the last four." Bill's voice, as he refers to the years
Jim has spent in pain and chemotherapy, is full of relief and love. "Just
to see you spry and jumping around, that is worth more than any of
the money we made," he says. "That money doesn't mean a thing."
Jim's son, Todd, gazes across the table at his father and then lowers his
eyes to his lap. Jim pauses, looks at his son, at Bill, stares into his coffee. The waitress reappears to collect the dishes. It starts to rain.

Carole too looks tired, her eyes especially. Every year when the sale
is over, after the months of long days, of having so many hands around
the ranch that their quiet life is almost forgotten, Bill looks at her with
awe and appreciation. It is not that he didn't expect this of her; it is that
he cannot believe they have accomplished the task again, that they
have come this far.

U

It is only the end of May, and a busy summer lies ahead. Most of the
sale crew heads home the morning after, and Bill and Carole get a few
nights' rest before starting nineteen colts in their first clinic of the summer in Chugwater, Wyoming. From there they head to ranches in
Colorado, Kansas, Vermont, Alabama, Texas, Nebraska, and Montana. Meanwhile, horses are being bought and hauled back to Thermopolis for next year's sale. By midsummer the herd will be assembled, working the West as pickup horses, ranch horses, cow horses,
packhorses, and hunters.

In August, Bill finally takes a vacation. Every year since he rode behind his father on the back of a packhorse, he has spent several weeks
in late summer deep in the Beartooth Mountains. He takes his horses
and his friends, and they ride and fish and play cards. It is by far his fa-

vorite time of year, and he waits for it with the impatience of a child. "They call them fishing trips, but they don't really do much fishing," says Ned Londo's son, Ben, who has joined the annual crew a few times. They ride and visit and relax, but mostly they ride. Bill never misses his summer trip to the mountains; he says there is nothing that will stop him from going.

"He loves them mountains," one friend said, "figures they're his." Opening a map on his kitchen table, Bill rubs a forefinger over the contours of the mountains south and east of Granite Peak, along the Montana-Wyoming border, just north of the Beartooth Highway.

"This is my territory," he says.

Some say Bill goes to the mountains because they are a good memory of his childhood. Others say he goes because it's wild, maybe the only wild place left. The land is rugged, untamed, and unforgiving. "I know he goes back because in those mountains you find the kind of peace you have when you're a kid," said his niece Lori, who has traveled with him for many years. Bill says he goes because it's pretty, and because he likes to be with his horses in the environment that is most natural to them, where they can be most free.

He usually heads out from Clay Butte, north of Cody just before Clark, with a string of thirty horses, riding some and packing the others with tents, food, and supplies. They ride fifteen, thirty, fifty miles into the mountains—wherever the meadows are clear and the footing is solid. In late summer they might still run into snow; the rivers might still be high with melt. All along the way they talk and sing songs and tell jokes, following unmarked trails that Glenn and Harry Smith broke.

The horses carry their riders through rivers and across meadows, up steep hills and through thick stands of trees. They step nimbly over the rocks, carefully picking their way. Horseshoes fall off and are replaced. Trees are felled, roped, dallied, and dragged into camp for firewood. Strings of brook and cutthroat trout are reeled out of the lake, battered in cornmeal, fried, and eaten. The fish are descendants of the fry carried there in buckets by Earl, Lloyd, and Lewis Thiel. Earl's great-grandsons fish with his daughter Edna and her son Bill in Thiel Lake.

One of Bill's favorite camps borders a lake surrounded by mountains and a nearby meadow that is large enough to feed a good number of horses. In the meadow a speckling of granite boulders, many of which only show their tips above ground, make it look as if Mother Nature left this place in the middle of her play. The lake, when it is still, reflects the mountains that surround it. In the center of camp, a lean-to shelters benches around a fire pit where all the action, besides fishing and riding, takes place—the cooking, the card playing, and the storytelling. They call it the Liar's Fire, the fire around which lies are told—lies or tales, depending on your definition and how much you can get away with. They are tales of great horses bred and born, of cowboys made and broken, of lives well lived.

Postscript

In October of 2000, with his friends and family forming the largest crowd for an inductee ever recorded, Bill Smith was inducted into the Rodeo Hall of Fame at the National Cowboy and Western Heritage Museum in Oklahoma City.

Notes

Chapter 1

3   *cost of raising them*   Jimmy Muse (ranch manager, the Bartlett Ranch), conversation with the author, Chugwater, Wyo., 2002.

9   *"this cowboy's only pay"*   Attributed to Cy Taillon, qtd. in Cyra McFadden's memoir of her father, McFadden, *Rain or Shine*, 15.

9   *"a little encouragement"*   Ibid.

11   *"like dancing with a girl"*   "Champ Rider," 123.

12   *Six feet two inches tall*   ProRodeo Sports News, *Rodeo Annual*, 107.

13   *cut the cinch*   Permanent collection, Professional Rodeo Cowboys Association Hall of Fame Museum, Colorado Springs, Colo.

15   *bone-busting brawls*   Axline, "Bearcreek, Montana."

16   *"Hands in your pockets"*   Adams, *Cowboy Lingo*, 190.

16   *When it was over*   Edna Smith, interview with the author, Cody, Wyo., November 4, 2000.

16   *built, boomed, and busted*   Cenis, "History of Bearcreek."

17   *"as Wild West as you could get"*   Jim Houston, telephone interview with the author, March 2001.

17   *Edna took a job*   Edna Smith interview.

Chapter 2

19   *never stop trying*   Wooden and Ehringer, *Rodeo in America*, 7–16.

19   *distinct vocabulary*   Adams, *Cowboy Lingo*, 98–105.

20   *unique talent*   Wooden and Ehringer, *Rodeo in America*, 7–16.

21   *return the favor*   Ibid.

21   *the real cowboy played himself*   Ibid.

22   *Pendleton, population 5,000*   Taylor and Marr, *American Cowboy*, 150.

22   *national scoring system*   Wooden and Ehringer, *Rodeo in America*, 7–16.

22   *land of opportunity*   Fredriksson, *American Rodeo*, 67.

23   *heroic only on a small scale*   Wooden and Ehringer, *Rodeo in America*, 223–24.

23   *"hind ends busted"*   Bill Smith, interview with the author, Thermopolis, Wyo., November 4–10, 2000   .

24   *Every night Bill worked*   Merle Fayles, interview with the author, Thermpolis, Wyo., November 4, 2000   .

25   *"pop your gizzard or eat dirt"*   "Champ Rider," 123–27.

26   *"He wasn't bad"*   Don Harrington, conversation with the author, Oklahoma City, Okla., October 20, 2006.

30   *"don't amount to nothin'"*   Fayles interview.

Chapter 3

36   *They listened*   German, *America's Music*, 41–54.

44   *"It's not a question"*   Wooden and Ehringer, *Rodeo in America*, 50.

44   *"not let it bother you"*   Fredriksson, *American Rodeo*, 133.

45   *seal signified*   *Cowboy Clothing and Gear*, introduction and 34.

46   *test of time*   Jim Wise, interview with the author, Loveland, Colo., June 2002.

46   *Up until that point*   Rattenbury, *Arena Legacy*.

46   *cowboys went on strike*   Jordan, *Rodeo History and Legends*, 76.

46   *cowboys everywhere*   Rattenbury, *Arena Legacy*.

46   *new specifications*   Wise interview.

47   *contents of his tack trailer*   Ibid.

47   *Roy Acuff sang*   Carson Robinson, "Railroad Boomer," performed by Roy Acuff and His Smokey Mountain Boys, *Country Music South and West*, New World Records sound recording NW287, 1977. Roy Acuff made this recording in 1939; the Country Music South and West album was released in 1977.

Chapter 4

48   *almost any other genre*   Wooden and Ehringer, *Rodeo in America*, 224–25.

50   *lucky shirts*   *San Francisco Chronicle*, October 23, 1962, 18.

54   *a good city for him*   Reid and Demaris, *Green Felt Jungle*, 144–77.

54   *"a most artistic way"*   McManus, *Positively Fifth Street*, 51.

58   *"riding easy in a rocking-chair"*   James, "Bucking Horses," 299.

59 *"Horses that buck"* Professional Rodeo Cowboys Association, *Official Pro Rodeo Media Guide 1978*, 97.

Chapter 5

61 *more than 450 women* Wooden and Ehringer, *Rodeo in America*, 188.
61 *followed Pendleton's lead* Rattenbury, *Arena Legacy*.
61 *"consistently ignored pleas"* LeCompte, *Cowgirls of the Rodeo*, 95–97.
61 *disinterest took a toll* Rattenbury, *Arena Legacy*.
61 *"glamorous lady riders"* Ibid.
62 *still not a Finals event* Wooden and Ehringer, *Rodeo in America*, 189.
62 *by marriage* A woman could win a gold buckle at a GRA rodeo but not at the National Finals.
63 *Let me guess* Toni Young, telephone interview, November 29, 2006.
64 *ten-day competition* *San Francisco Chronicle*, October 24, 1964, 12.
65 *"she said okay and saved me"* "Executive Order 11119 (September 10, 1963) changed Selective Service System regulations. Married men without children were placed one step lower in the order of call than single men." Selective Service System, "Effects of Marriage and Fatherhood on Draft Eligibility," July 9, 2003, http://www.sss.gov/FSeffects.htm.
71 *"most imitated styles"* Professional Rodeo Cowboys Association, "Legend Bill Smith Says Goodbye," news release, April 23, 1979.
73 *most money at the end of the year* Fredriksson, *American Rodeo*, 96–97.
73 *a world series of rodeo* Ibid.
74 *fancy buckskin chaps* Bill's new chaps were made by the seamstress Marge Taylor. His old chaps were borrowed by Larry Mahan, who won his first all-around title wearing them. They were later worn by Rick Smith and eventually given to Todd Ficke.
75 *Bucking Horse of the Year* ProRodeo Sports News, *1963 Rodeo Annual*, 48; ProRodeo Sports News, *1964 Rodeo Annual*, 64.

76   *impressive and memorable*   ProRodeo Sports News, *1966 Rodeo Annual,* 83.

76   *margin of less than $700*   Professional Rodeo Cowboys Association, *Finals,* 1965 section.

Chapter 6

77   *frightneningly large*   Permanent collection, Professional Rodeo Cowboys Association Hall of Fame Museum, Colorado Springs, Colo.

78   *several hundred freed slaves*   White, "Paul Stewart Mines," 66.

78   *twenty-four-year-old drifter*   "8 Student Nurses Slain," *New York Times,* July 14, 1966.

Chapter 7

91   *for a moment*   Russ Taylor, "Bill Smith in National Saddle Bronc Finals," *Cody Enterprise,* December 3, 1969, 1.

92   *He won $918*   Ibid., 8.

93   *three weeks earlier*   Bill Smith, interview with the author, Thermopolis, Wyo., November 4–10, 2000 .

94   *Bill was still $3,847 ahead*   Ibid.

100   *only five men had managed it*   Westermeier, *Man, Beast, Dust,* 420–21.

101   *didn't believe in divorce*   Toni Young, telephone interview with the author, November 29, 2006.

Chapter 8

109   *Buck was fast*   The all-around cowgirl title includes barrel racing and goat tying events.

113   *Bill closed his season*   Professional Rodeo Cowboys Association, *Finals,* 1973 section.

115   *staging ground for troops*   Jordan, *Rodeo History and Legends,* 50.

Chapter 9

123 *Walt Garrison* Ned Londo, interview with the author, Las Vegas, Nev., December 2000. Separately, Walt Garrison himself tells a story about Bill riding his horse twenty miles out of his hunting camp and renting a motel room in town just to watch a Cowboys game, in *Once a Cowboy*, 175.

125 *"Twice in my life"* Fredriksson, *American Rodeo*, 125.

Chapter 10

132 *top fifteen bronc riders* Bill Smith, interview with the author, Thermopolis, Wyo., November 4–10, 2000 .

134 *crowd was on its feet* Video recording of Copenhagen-Skoal Championship 1978. Collection of Bill Smith, Thermopolis, Wyo.

134 *"still an aspiration"* "Rodeo Superstars Championship," *Western Horseman*, 53–54.

137 *last ride of his career* Bill Smith interview.

Chapter 11

141 *"never rode a broke horse"* Hunt, *Think Harmony*, 1–68. This dialogue of Ray Hunt speaking is taken directly from his book on the subject of horsemanship and is, as Bill Smith remembers it, accurate as to the experience he had at his first clinic.

146 *distinguished clientele* Though this story was never corroborated, it was told to me in an interview with Jack "Sundown" Wipplinger, in Red Lodge, Mont., June 28, 2002.

Chapter 12

156 *"formed from violence"* Sylvia Livingston, interview with the author, Thermopolis, Wyo., July 2002.

156 *"dynamited that road"* Ibid.

157 *"burn that house down"* Ibid.

159 *most popular horses in the West* "The American Quarter Horse," American Quarter Horse Association, http://www.aqha.com/ association/who/thehorse.html.

160   *average price*   Carole Smith, interview with the author,
       Thermopolis, Wyo., July 2001.

163   *"rather have the horse"*   Bill Smith, interview with the author,
       Thermopolis, Wyo., November 4–10, 2000   .

169   *"don't really do much fishing"*   Ben Londo, conversation with the
       author, Thermopolis, Wyo., May 2001.

169   *"kind of peace"*   Lori Coy, interview with the author, Cody, Wyo.,
       May 2001.

Bibliography

Published Sources

Adams, Ramon F. *Cowboy Lingo*. Boston: Houghton Mifflin, 1936.

Ahlborn, Richard E., ed. *Man Made Mobile: Early Saddles of Western North America*. New York: Smithsonian Institution Press, 1980.

Allen, Michael. *Rodeo Cowboys in the North American Imagination*. Reno: University of Nevada Press, 1998.

Anderson, Bob. *Beartooth Country: Montana's Absaroka and Beartooth Mountains*. Helena: Montana Magazine/American and World Geographic Publishing, 1994.

Axline, Jon. "Bearcreek, Montana." *Montana The Magazine of Western History* 54, no. 3 (Autumn 2004): 74.

Cenis, Bill. "History of Bearcreek: The Town That Refuses to Fade Away." June 2006. http://www.bearcreekmt.com/history/htm.

"Champ Rider." *Life Magazine*. October 22, 1951. 123–27.

Cowboy Clothing and Gear: The Complete Hamley Catalog of 1942. New York: Dover, 1995.

Crawford, William. *The Bronc Rider*. New York: Ballantine Books, 1965.

Dary, David. *Cowboy Culture: A Saga of Five Centuries*. New York: Alfred A. Knopf, 1981.

Fredriksson, Kristine. *American Rodeo: From Buffalo Bill to Big Business*. College Station: Texas A&M Universtiy Press, 1985.

Garrison, Walt. *Once a Cowboy*. New York: Random House, 1988.

German, Robert K. *America's Music: The Roots of Country*. Atlanta: Turner Publishing, 1996.

"Getting in Step with Dad." *Sports Illustrated*, October 4, 1976, 44.

"Great Bronc Riders Think Harmony with Horses." *Quarter Horse Journal* (December 1997): 52–55.

Hunt, Ray. *Think Harmony with Horses: An In-Depth Study of the Horse/Man Relationship*. 1978. Reprint, Sanger, Calif.: Quill Driver Books, 1991.

Hussa, Linda. *Lige Langston: Sweet Langston*. Tulsa: University of Oklahoma, 1999.

James, Will. "Bucking Horses and Bucking Horse Riders." *Scribner's Magazine*. 73, no. 3 (March 1923): 297–305.

——. *Cowboys North and South*. Missoula: Mountain Press Publishing, 1996.

——. *Lone Cowboy*. Missoula: Mountain Press Publishing, 1996.

Johnson, Dirk. *Biting the Dust: The Wild Ride and Dark Romance of the Rodeo Cowboy and the American West*. New York: Simon and Schuster, 1994.

Jordan, Bob. *Rodeo History and Legends*. Montrose, Colo.: Rodeo Stuff, 1994.

Kuhlman, Fay, and Gary Robson. *The Darkest Hour: A Comprehensive Account of the Smith Mine Disaster of 1943*. 2nd ed. Red Lodge, Mont.: Red Lodge Books, 2003.

Lawrence, Elizabeth Atwood. *Rodeo: An Anthropologist Looks at the Wild and the Tame*. Knoxville: University of Tennesse Press, 1982.

LeCompte, Mary Lou. *Cowgirls of the Rodeo*. Chicago: University of Illinois Press, 1993.

Lindmier, Tom, and Steve Mount. *I Can See by Your Outfit: Historic Cowboy Gear of the Northern Plains*. Glendo, Wyo.: High Plains Press, 1996.

Lofting, Colin. "How to Win Money on a Horse." *Saturday Evening Post*, August 25, 1956, 32, 33, 84–86.

Luebke, Frederick, ed. *European Immigrants in the American West: Community Histories*. Albuquerque: University of New Mexico Press, 1998.

McFadden, Cyra. *Rain or Shine: A Family Memoir*. New York: Knopf, 1986.

McManus, James. *Positively Fifth Street: Murderers, Cheetahs, and Binion's World Series of Poker*. New York: Farrar, Straus, Giroux, 2003.

Miller, Robert M. *Understanding the Ancient Secrets of the Horse's Mind*. Neenah: Russell Meerdink, 1999.

Professional Rodeo Cowboys Association. *The Finals: A Complete History of the National Finals Rodeo*. Colorado Springs: Professional Rodeo Cowboys Association, 1998.

——. *Official Pro Rodeo Media Guide 1978*. Colorado Springs: Professional Rodeo Cowboys Association, 1978.

ProRodeo Sports News. *Rodeo Annual*. January 1962.

Rattenbury, Richard C. *Arena Legacy: The Rodeo Collections of the National Cowboy and Western Heritage Museum*. Norman: University of Oklahoma Press, forthcoming.

"Red Lodge Rodeo a Community Asset: Officers and Directors Inclue Many Prominent Business Men of City." *Official Program of the Red Lodge Rodeo,* 1933.

Reid, Ed, and Ovid Demaris. *The Green Felt Jungle.* Cutchogue, N.Y.: Buccaneer Books, 1963.

"Rodeo Superstars Championship." *Western Horseman,* July 1979, 53–54.

"Rookie of the Year." *1963 Rodeo Sports News Rodeo Annual* 11, no. 3 (January 1963): 53.

Sedgwick. "Once Horse People, Always Horse People." *Wyoming Wrangler* 2, no. 8 (February 1989): 1.

"Starting Colts with Bill Smith." *Western Horseman,* January 1999, 64–74.

Slatta, Richard W. *Cowboys of the Americas.* New Haven: Yale University Press, 1990.

Taylor, Lonn, and Ingrid Maar. *The American Cowboy.* Washington, D.C.: Library of Congress, 1983. (Exhibition catalog; reprint, New York: Harper and Row, 1983.)

Turner, Frederick Jackson. *The Frontier in American History.* New York: Henry Holt, 1920.

Westermeier, Clifford P. *Man, Beast, Dust: The Story of Rodeo.* Lincoln: University of Nebraska Press, 1947.

A Western Legacy: The National Cowboy and Western Heritage Museum. Norman: University of Oklahoma Press, 2005.

White, Evelyn C. "How Paul Stewart Mines Lost 'Gold' with a Tape Recorder." *Smithsonian Magazine,* August 1989, 58–68.

Witte, Randy. "Bill Smith on Saddle Bronc Riding." *Western Horseman,* November 1979, 14–18.

Wooden, Wayne S., and Gavin Ehringer. *Rodeo in America: Wranglers, Roughstock, and Paydirt.* Lawrence: University of Kansas Press, 1996.

Interviews

Bartlett, Woodrow. Interviews with the author, various dates, May 2001, Thermopolis, Wyo.; June 2002, Chugwater, Wyo.

Coy, B. Joe. Interviews with the author, various dates, May 2001, Thermopolis and Cody, Wyo.

Coy, Lori Smith. Interviews with the author, November 4, 2000, Cody, Wyo.; various dates, July 2001, Thermopolis and Cody, Wyo.

Fales, Merle. Interview with the author, November 5, 2000, Thermopolis, Wyo.

Ficke, Jim. Interviews with the author, November 10, 2000, Riverton, Wyo.; May 20, 2001, Thermopolis, Wyo.

Ficke, Diane Smith. Interview with the author, November 10, 2000, Riverton, Wyo.

Frost, Clyde. Interview with the author, December 8, 2000, Las Vegas, Nev.

Harrington, Don. Interview with the author, October 20, 2006, Oklahoma City, Okla.

Houston, Jim. Telephone interview with the author, December 2000.

Hyland, Mel. Interviews with the author, various dates, May 2001, Thermopolis, Wyo.; October 20–21, 2006, Oklahoma City, Okla.

Jones, Ken. Interviews with the author, various dates, June 2000, Clark, Colo.; November 2000, Las Vegas, Nev.; May 2001, Thermopolis, Wyo.

Kesler, Reg. Interview with the author, December 8, 2000, Las Vegas, Nev.

Livingston, Sylvia. Interviews with the author, various dates, July 2002, Thermopolis, Wyo.

Londo, Ned. Interview with the author, December 21, 2000, Thermopolis, Wyo.

Mahan, Larry. Interview with the author, October 20, 2006, Oklahoma City, Okla.

McSpadden, Clem. Interview with the author, October 20, 2006, Oklahoma City, Okla.

Mitner, Suzi. Interview with the author, November 4, 2000, Cody, Wyo.

O'Rourke, Jaime. Interview with the author, December 9, 2000, Las Vegas, Nev.

O'Rourke, Reid. Interview with the author, November 9, 2000, Thermopolis, Wyo.

Reid, Barbara Smith. Interview with the author, November 4, 2000, Cody, Wyo.

Smith, Bill. Interviews with the author, various dates, 2000–2006, Chugwater, Riverton, and Thermoplis, Wyo.; Las Vegas, Nev.; Oklahoma City, Okla.

Smith, Carole O'Rourke. Interviews with the author, various dates, 2000–2006, Chugwater, Cody, Riverton, and Thermopolis, Wyo.; Las Vegas, Nev.; Oklahoma City, Okla.

Smith, Edna. Interviews with the author, November 4, 2000, Cody, Wyo.; July 2002, Cody, Wyo.

Smith, Rick. Interviews with the author, December 8, 2000, Las Vegas, Nev.; various dates 2000–2006, Thermopolis and Chugwater, Wyo.

Swanson, Chuck. Interviews with the author, various dates, March 2001, Thermopolis, Wyo.

Wipplinger, Eileen Smith. Interview with the author, November 10, 2000, Cody, Wyo.

Wipplinger, Jack "Sundown." Interview with the author, June 28, 2002, Red Lodge, Mont.

Wise, Jim. Interview with the author, December 8, 2000, Loveland, Colo.

Young, Toni. Telephone interview with the author, November 29, 2006.

Acknowledgments

When he first agreed to tell me his life story, Bill Smith didn't know me any more than I knew him, any more than you know a person you just met. But he and Carole took me into their home, introduced me to family and friends, and reflected onto the glossy spools of 120-minute tape memories of childhood, young adulthood, and married and working life. I am thankful for their generosity, and for their confidence. Family, friends, acquaintances, and strangers shared with me their impressions, opinions, stories, and thoughts, let me hang around, put me up, and gave me a horse to ride. More often than not it was in the action, the activities, and the informal conversations that the grit of this story was gotten, where the true characters were revealed, and I owe to everyone who let me ride beside them my deepest appreciation and my thanks.

I also owe a very special thanks to Patricia O'Toole for her mentorship, insight, good advice, and friendship; to Richard Locke, Rob Farnsworth, Peter Scott, and Mark Spragg for their ears, eyes, and encouragement; and to everyone who read draft after draft, especially Elizabeth Angell, Eva Blank, Emily Bliss, Ellen Bresler, Scott Case, Dan Browne, Elyssa East, Liz Entman, Olivia Gentile, Amy Greene, Stephen Johnson, Jessica Ludders, Suzanne Menghraj, John O'Connor, Amanda Petrusich, Jessica Roake, Brian Seibert, Jen Shotz, Dustin Beale Smith, and Griff Witte.

I am most grateful to the librarians at the Seattle Public Library, the Columbia University Library, and the Park County Historical Archives in Cody, Wyoming, who were amazingly tenacious and obliging. At the National Cowboy and Western Heritage Museum in Oklahoma City, Chuck Shroeder was ever gracious, and Chuck Rand's and Richard Rattenbury's assistance were instrumental in helping me sort out my facts. The Ohioana Library Association awarded me a generous boost of confidence at just the right time, which was a true gift. Renae Morehead was careful and kind with her red pencil, and Steven Baker should be awarded the golden gloves award for manuscript editors, if there is such a thing; I feel fortunate for having had him in my corner. Finally, I am ever grateful to Chuck Rankin at the University of Oklahoma Press for believing in this book.

Index